THIS BELONGS TO:

←——————————————————→

INTRODUCTION: A COMPANION TO YOUR CALLING

WELCOME TO THE 30-DAY DEVOTIONAL JOURNAL! THIS JOURNAL GOES ALONG WITH JOSEPH & MARKETPLACE MINISTRY: A SIMPLE GUIDE TO KINGDOM LEADERSHIP. IT'S MADE TO HELP YOU GO DEEPER INTO THE LESSONS OF LEADERSHIP FOUND IN JOSEPH'S STORY. WHETHER YOU'RE A PASTOR, BUSINESS LEADER, STUDENT, OR SOMEONE WHO WANTS TO LIVE OUT GOD'S PURPOSE, THIS DEVOTIONAL IS FOR YOU.

JOSEPH'S STORY IN GENESIS 37–50 ISN'T JUST HISTORY—IT'S A GUIDE FOR LEADING WITH FAITH, HANDLING HARD TIMES, MANAGING RESOURCES WELL, AND USING YOUR INFLUENCE THE RIGHT WAY. THIS JOURNAL WILL HELP YOU LEARN FROM JOSEPH ONE DAY AT A TIME AND TURN THOSE LESSONS INTO REAL GROWTH IN YOUR LIFE.

EACH DAY, YOU'LL READ A SHORT DEVOTIONAL, THINK ABOUT THE BIBLE, TALK WITH GOD, AND TAKE STEPS TO LIVE OUT YOUR PURPOSE. GET READY TO GROW, LEAD WITH COURAGE, AND MAKE A DIFFERENCE WHEREVER GOD HAS PLACED YOU!

HOW TO USE THIS JOURNAL

THIS DEVOTIONAL IS INTENDED TO BE USED ALONGSIDE THE BOOK JOSEPH & MARKETPLACE MINISTRY: A SIMPLE GUIDE TO KINGDOM LEADERSHIP. EACH CHAPTER OF THE BOOK PROVIDES THE FOUNDATION, AND THIS JOURNAL OFFERS A SPACE TO REFLECT, RESPOND, AND GROW IN ALIGNMENT WITH THE KEY LESSONS FROM EACH SECTION.

EACH DAY'S DEVOTIONAL INCLUDES:

SCRIPTURE FOCUS

A BIBLE VERSE THAT ANCHORS THE DAY'S THEME AND PREPARES YOUR HEART FOR REFLECTION.

DEVOTIONAL READING

A SHORT, EASY-TO-READ REFLECTION THAT CONNECTS JOSEPH'S STORY TO YOUR PERSONAL LEADERSHIP AND FAITH JOURNEY.

REFLECTION QUESTIONS

PROMPTS TO HELP YOU APPLY BIBLICAL TRUTH TO YOUR REAL-LIFE CIRCUMSTANCES, DECISIONS, AND RELATIONSHIPS.

FAITH STEPS

PRACTICAL, ACTIONABLE STEPS THAT HELP YOU MOVE FROM INSPIRATION TO TRANSFORMATION.

PRAYER

A CLOSING PRAYER TO HELP YOU ALIGN YOUR HEART AND LEADERSHIP WITH GOD'S WILL.

HOW TO GET THE MOST OUT OF THIS DEVOTIONAL

- **GO SLOW:** READ ONE DEVOTIONAL EACH DAY. TAKE TIME TO THINK AND LET GOD SPEAK TO YOUR HEART.

- **WRITE IT DOWN:** USE THE REFLECTION QUESTIONS TO HELP YOU JOURNAL OR TALK TO GOD IN PRAYER.

- **GROW WITH OTHERS:** YOU CAN GO THROUGH THIS DEVOTIONAL WITH A FRIEND, MENTOR, OR LEADERSHIP GROUP.

- **READ AGAIN LATER:** THESE LESSONS CAN MEAN DIFFERENT THINGS IN DIFFERENT SEASONS. COME BACK TO THEM AS YOU GROW.

THIS ISN'T JUST A BOOK TO READ—IT'S A TOOL TO HELP YOU LEAD WITH PURPOSE. AS YOU WALK THROUGH THESE 30 DAYS, MAY YOU CARRY THE SPIRIT OF JOSEPH—TO DREAM BIG, LEAD STRONG, AND WALK BOLDLY IN THE PLACE GOD HAS CALLED YOU.

"BUT AS FOR YOU, YOU MEANT EVIL AGAINST ME; BUT GOD MEANT IT FOR GOOD, IN ORDER TO BRING IT ABOUT AS IT IS THIS DAY, TO SAVE MANY PEOPLE ALIVE."

– GENESIS 50:20 (NKJV)

DEVOTIONAL READING

JOSEPH'S STORY BEGINS WITH BETRAYAL AND PAIN, BUT THAT'S NOT HOW IT ENDS. HIS BROTHERS HATED HIM, SOLD HIM INTO SLAVERY, AND TRIED TO ERASE HIM FROM THEIR LIVES. BUT GOD HAD A GREATER PLAN. EVEN WHEN THINGS LOOKED BROKEN, GOD WAS USING EVERY STEP TO BRING JOSEPH CLOSER TO HIS PURPOSE.

SOMETIMES LIFE FEELS UNFAIR. YOU MAY FACE REJECTION, FAILURE, OR DELAYS THAT DON'T MAKE SENSE. BUT GOD IS NOT SURPRISED BY YOUR PAIN—HE'S WORKING THROUGH IT. LIKE JOSEPH, YOUR JOURNEY HAS A PURPOSE THAT GOES BEYOND YOUR PRESENT SITUATION.

JOSEPH STAYED FAITHFUL, EVEN WHEN LIFE FELT UNFAIR. HIS STORY REMINDS US THAT GOD CAN USE EVEN THE WORST MOMENTS TO LEAD US INTO SOMETHING GREATER. WHEN WE TRUST GOD THROUGH THE HARD TIMES, HE TURNS PAIN INTO PURPOSE AND TRIALS INTO TESTIMONIES.

Today,

**HAVE YOU EVER
EXPERIENCED
SOMETHING PAINFUL
THAT LATER MADE YOU
STRONGER?**

_____
_____
_____
_____
_____
_____
_____
_____
_____

Today,

**HOW CAN YOU
CHOOSE FAITH AND
HOPE EVEN WHEN
THINGS DON'T GO
YOUR WAY?**

_____
_____
_____
_____
_____
_____
_____
_____
_____

FAITH IN MOTION

Faith in Motion

Today,

WRITE DOWN ONE CHALLENGE YOU'RE FACING TODAY AND ASK GOD TO SHOW YOU HOW HE MIGHT USE IT FOR GOOD.

Today,

PRAY OVER IT DAILY THIS WEEK, ASKING GOD TO GIVE YOU WISDOM AND STRENGTH TO GROW INTO IT.

GOD'S PRESENCE IS YOUR GREATEST ADVANTAGE—CARRY IT WITH YOU EVERYWHERE.

SCRIPTURE MEDITATION

"AND WE KNOW THAT ALL THINGS WORK TOGETHER FOR GOOD TO THOSE WHO LOVE GOD, TO THOSE WHO ARE THE CALLED ACCORDING TO HIS PURPOSE."
–ROMANS 8:28 (NKJV)

MEDITATION REFLECTION

WHEN LIFE FEELS UNFAIR, IT'S EASY TO DOUBT GOD'S PLAN. BUT ROMANS 8:28 REMINDS US THAT GOD WORKS ALL THINGS TOGETHER FOR GOOD–EVEN BETRAYAL, SETBACKS, AND PAIN. LIKE JOSEPH, WE CAN HOLD ON TO FAITH, KNOWING THAT EVERY TRIAL IS PART OF A GREATER PURPOSE. TRUSTING GOD IN HARDSHIP SHAPES US FOR THE BLESSINGS AHEAD.

KEY POINTS

- GOD CAN REDEEM EVERY BROKEN PART OF YOUR STORY.
- FAITH DURING TRIALS LEADS TO PURPOSE AND TESTIMONY.
- GOD'S PLAN IS BIGGER THAN YOUR PAIN.

DEAR GOD,

THANK YOU FOR BEING WITH ME IN EVERY SEASON—EVEN THE HARD ONES. HELP ME TO TRUST YOU WHEN LIFE FEELS CONFUSING OR PAINFUL. REMIND ME THAT YOU ARE ALWAYS WORKING BEHIND THE SCENES FOR MY GOOD. GIVE ME THE STRENGTH TO STAY FAITHFUL AND THE COURAGE TO WALK FORWARD WITH HOPE.

IN JESUS' NAME, AMEN.

JOURNAL REFLECTION-NEXT STEPS
Journal Reflection-Next Steps

"THEN PHARAOH SAID TO JOSEPH, 'INASMUCH AS GOD HAS SHOWN YOU ALL THIS, THERE IS NO ONE AS DISCERNING AND WISE AS YOU. YOU SHALL BE OVER MY HOUSE, AND ALL MY PEOPLE SHALL BE RULED ACCORDING TO YOUR WORD.'"

– GENESIS 41:39–40 (NKJV)

DEVOTIONAL READING

JOSEPH DIDN'T CHASE POWER—HE WALKED WITH GOD. EVEN IN PRISON, HE SERVED FAITHFULLY AND STAYED CONNECTED TO GOD'S VOICE. WHEN THE TIME CAME, GOD PROMOTED HIM. IT WASN'T JOSEPH'S PLAN THAT LED HIM TO LEADERSHIP—IT WAS HIS OBEDIENCE, CHARACTER, AND WISDOM.

THIS REMINDS US THAT PURPOSE IS NOT ABOUT POSITION—IT'S ABOUT PREPARATION. JOSEPH'S CALLING WASN'T ABOUT BEING FAMOUS; IT WAS ABOUT SAVING LIVES. YOUR CALLING MAY NOT LOOK LIKE SOMEONE ELSE'S, BUT IT MATTERS DEEPLY TO GOD. HE HAS PLACED YOU WHERE YOU ARE FOR A REASON.

WHEN WE LIVE ON PURPOSE, WE REFLECT GOD'S KINGDOM IN OUR SCHOOLS, FAMILIES, AND WORKPLACES. YOU WERE CREATED TO INFLUENCE YOUR WORLD WITH FAITH, INTEGRITY, AND LOVE. LIKE JOSEPH, WHEN YOU STAY FAITHFUL, GOD WILL OPEN DOORS AT THE RIGHT TIME.

Today,

WHERE HAS GOD PLACED YOU RIGHT NOW TO MAKE A DIFFERENCE?

Today,

WHAT GIFTS OR TALENTS CAN YOU USE TO SERVE OTHERS TODAY?

FAITH IN MOTION
Faith in Motion

Today,

**WRITE A SHORT
PURPOSE STATEMENT:
WHY DO YOU BELIEVE
GOD MADE YOU?**

_____
_____
_____
_____
_____
_____
_____
_____
_____
_____

Today,

**FIND ONE SMALL WAY
TO SERVE SOMEONE
THIS WEEK—AT
SCHOOL, WORK, OR
HOME.**

_____
_____
_____
_____
_____
_____
_____
_____
_____
_____

**FAITHFULNESS IN SMALL THINGS
OPENS DOORS TO GREATER
THINGS.**

SCRIPTURE MEDITATION

"FOR WE ARE HIS WORKMANSHIP, CREATED IN CHRIST JESUS FOR GOOD WORKS, WHICH GOD PREPARED BEFOREHAND THAT WE SHOULD WALK IN THEM."
—EPHESIANS 2:10 (NKJV)

MEDITATION REFLECTION

YOU WERE NOT MADE BY ACCIDENT. GOD HANDCRAFTED YOU WITH INTENTION AND PLACED YOU IN THIS GENERATION FOR GOOD WORKS. LIKE JOSEPH, YOUR PATH MAY BE UNEXPECTED, BUT YOUR PURPOSE IS SECURE. EVERY STEP OF OBEDIENCE BRINGS YOU CLOSER TO THE IMPACT GOD DESIGNED YOU TO HAVE.

KEY POINTS

- YOUR CALLING IS UNIQUELY CRAFTED BY GOD.
- OBEDIENCE UNLOCKS THE DOORS TO PURPOSE.
- WHERE YOU ARE NOW IS PART OF YOUR ASSIGNMENT.

FATHER,
THANK YOU FOR CREATING
ME WITH PURPOSE. HELP
ME TO WALK IN
OBEDIENCE, JUST LIKE
JOSEPH. GIVE ME WISDOM
FOR TODAY AND FAITH FOR
TOMORROW. USE MY LIFE
TO BLESS OTHERS AND
BUILD YOUR KINGDOM. IN
JESUS' NAME, AMEN.

JOURNAL REFLECTION-NEXT STEPS
Journal Reflection-Next Steps

"WHERE THERE IS NO VISION, THE PEOPLE PERISH: BUT HE THAT KEEPETH THE LAW, HAPPY IS HE."

— PROVERBS 29:18 (KJV)

WHEN GOD PLACES A DREAM IN YOUR HEART, IT MAY FEEL EXCITING—BUT ALSO UNCERTAIN. LIKE JOSEPH, YOU MAY NOT HAVE ALL THE STEPS FIGURED OUT, BUT THAT DOESN'T MEAN THE VISION ISN'T REAL. GOD OFTEN SHOWS US THE END BEFORE REVEALING THE MIDDLE. THE VISION IS A SPARK THAT LIGHTS THE PATH, EVEN WHEN THE JOURNEY IS LONG.

JOSEPH DIDN'T UNDERSTAND WHY HE WAS SOLD BY HIS BROTHERS OR THROWN INTO PRISON, BUT HE NEVER LET GO OF THE DREAM. HE TRUSTED THAT GOD HAD A BIGGER PLAN EVEN WHEN THINGS DIDN'T MAKE SENSE. THAT'S THE KIND OF TRUST GOD WANTS FROM US. WHEN YOU HOLD ON TO THE VISION THROUGH HARD TIMES, YOU GROW STRONGER AND MORE PREPARED FOR WHAT'S COMING.

Today,

**WHAT IS ONE DREAM
YOU BELIEVE GOD HAS
PLACED IN YOUR
HEART?**

_____
_____
_____
_____
_____
_____

Today,

**HOW HAVE DELAYS OR
SETBACKS MADE YOU
DOUBT THAT DREAM?**

_____
_____
_____
_____
_____
_____

Today,

**WHAT WOULD IT LOOK
LIKE TO TRUST GOD
MORE FULLY WITH
THAT VISION?**

_____
_____
_____
_____
_____
_____

Today,

REVIEW YOUR JOURNAL OR NOTES TO FIND ANY DREAMS OR IDEAS THAT FEEL GOD-GIVEN.

Today,

CIRCLE OR HIGHLIGHT ONE THAT STILL STIRS YOUR HEART AND ASK GOD TO CONFIRM IT.

Today,

WRITE A PRAYER ASKING GOD TO RENEW YOUR TRUST AND GIVE YOU PEACE WHILE YOU WAIT.

YOU DON'T NEED A TITLE TO WALK IN PURPOSE.

SCRIPTURE MEDITATION

"COMMIT YOUR WORKS TO THE LORD, AND YOUR THOUGHTS
WILL BE ESTABLISHED."
–PROVERBS 16:3 (NKJV)

MEDITATION REFLECTION

VISIONS FROM GOD OFTEN COME BEFORE THE PATHWAY IS
CLEAR. COMMITTING YOUR DREAMS TO GOD BRINGS CLARITY
AND ALIGNMENT. JOSEPH DIDN'T GIVE UP WHEN THINGS DIDN'T
MAKE SENSE—HE STAYED CONNECTED TO THE VISION.
TRUSTING GOD'S PLAN MEANS SURRENDERING CONTROL
WHILE HOLDING ONTO HOPE.

KEY POINTS

- GOD REVEALS VISION IN STAGES—TRUST THE PROCESS.
- SURRENDER BRINGS CLARITY.
- DELAYS ARE NOT DENIALS—THEY'RE PREPARATION.

LORD,
THANK YOU FOR THE VISION
YOU'VE PLACED IN MY LIFE.
HELP ME TO HOLD ONTO IT,
EVEN WHEN THE PATH IS
UNCLEAR. GROW MY FAITH
THROUGH THE WAITING AND
SHAPE ME FOR WHAT'S AHEAD.
I TRUST THAT YOU ARE
WORKING BEHIND THE
SCENES, AND I CHOOSE TO
BELIEVE IN YOUR TIMING.
IN JESUS' NAME, AMEN.

JOURNAL REFLECTION-NEXT STEPS
Journal Reflection-Next Steps

_____
_____
_____
_____
_____
_____
_____
_____
_____
_____
_____
_____
_____
_____
_____
_____
_____
_____
_____
_____
_____
_____
_____
_____

"WRITE THE VISION AND MAKE IT PLAIN ON TABLETS, THAT HE MAY RUN WHO READS IT. FOR THE VISION IS YET FOR AN APPOINTED TIME... THOUGH IT TARRIES, WAIT FOR IT; BECAUSE IT WILL SURELY COME, IT WILL NOT TARRY."

— HABAKKUK 2:2–3 (NKJV)

JOSEPH'S JOURNEY REMINDS US THAT JUST BECAUSE A DREAM IS DELAYED DOESN'T MEAN IT'S DENIED. EVERY DELAY HAS A PURPOSE. IT'S EASY TO FEEL FORGOTTEN WHEN THINGS TAKE LONGER THAN WE HOPED, BUT GOD HASN'T ABANDONED YOUR VISION. HE IS USING THIS TIME TO GROW YOUR FAITH, DEVELOP YOUR CHARACTER, AND ALIGN THE RIGHT CIRCUMSTANCES.

GOD'S TIMING IS ALWAYS PERFECT. WHEN JOSEPH WAITED IN PRISON, HE COULD HAVE GIVEN UP—BUT HE STAYED FAITHFUL. YOUR WAITING SEASON IS NOT A WASTE. IT'S WHERE GOD DOES SOME OF HIS MOST IMPORTANT WORK IN YOU. WHEN THE TIME IS RIGHT, THE VISION WILL SPEAK—AND IT WILL BE WORTH THE WAIT.

DAILY REFLECTION
Daily Reflection

Today,

HOW DO YOU USUALLY RESPOND WHEN YOUR PLANS ARE DELAYED?

_____
_____
_____
_____
_____
_____

Today,

WHAT LESSON MIGHT GOD BE TEACHING YOU DURING THIS WAITING SEASON?

_____
_____
_____
_____
_____
_____

Today,

IS THERE SOMETHING HE WANTS TO DEVELOP IN YOUR CHARACTER BEFORE THE DREAM IS FULFILLED?

_____
_____
_____
_____

IDENTIFY ONE AREA WHERE YOU FEEL STUCK OR DELAYED.

_____
_____
_____
_____
_____
_____

ASK GOD TO HELP YOU SEE THE PURPOSE IN THIS PAUSE.

_____
_____
_____
_____
_____
_____

WRITE A SHORT NOTE TO YOURSELF ABOUT WHAT YOU'RE LEARNING AND HOW YOU'RE GROWING IN THE WAIT.

_____
_____
_____
_____
_____

GOD'S PRESENCE IS YOUR GREATEST ADVANTAGE—CARRY IT WITH YOU EVERYWHERE.

SCRIPTURE MEDITATION

"FOR THE LORD IS NOT SLACK CONCERNING HIS PROMISE, AS SOME COUNT SLACKNESS, BUT IS LONGSUFFERING TOWARD US…"
—2 PETER 3:9A (NKJV)

MEDITATION REFLECTION

DELAY DOESN'T MEAN GOD HAS FORGOTTEN. HE IS PATIENT AND PURPOSEFUL. JOSEPH'S YEARS IN PRISON WERE FILLED WITH DIVINE PREPARATION. GOD IS NEVER LATE—HE'S ALIGNING EVERYTHING FOR THE RIGHT MOMENT. WAITING BECOMES FRUITFUL WHEN WE LEAN ON HIS TIMING.

KEY POINTS

- DELAYS REFINE YOUR CHARACTER.
- GOD'S TIMING IS ALWAYS PERFECT.
- PATIENCE IS A SIGN OF SPIRITUAL MATURITY.

GOD,
I CONFESS THAT WAITING
CAN BE HARD. BUT I KNOW
YOU ARE DOING SOMETHING
GOOD IN ME, EVEN WHEN I
CAN'T SEE IT. HELP ME TO BE
PATIENT, STRONG, AND FULL
OF FAITH. TEACH ME WHAT I
NEED TO LEARN SO I'M READY
WHEN THE VISION COMES TO
PASS. I TRUST YOU WITH
EVERY STEP OF THIS
JOURNEY. IN JESUS' NAME,
AMEN.

JOURNAL REFLECTION-NEXT STEPS
Journal Reflection-Next Steps

"YOU ARE THE LIGHT OF THE WORLD. A CITY THAT IS SET ON A HILL CANNOT BE HIDDEN. NOR DO THEY LIGHT A LAMP AND PUT IT UNDER A BASKET, BUT ON A LAMPSTAND, AND IT GIVES LIGHT TO ALL WHO ARE IN THE HOUSE. LET YOUR LIGHT SO SHINE BEFORE MEN, THAT THEY MAY SEE YOUR GOOD WORKS AND GLORIFY YOUR FATHER IN HEAVEN."

—MATTHEW 5:14–16 (NKJV)

DEVOTIONAL READING

GOD PLACED YOU IN THIS WORLD TO MAKE A DIFFERENCE. JUST LIKE JOSEPH, YOU HAVE A LIGHT THAT CAN SHINE IN DARK PLACES. WHEN JOSEPH LED IN EGYPT, HE DIDN'T JUST WORK FOR SUCCESS—HE HELPED OTHERS AND FOLLOWED GOD'S WAYS. HIS LEADERSHIP SAVED LIVES AND BROUGHT PEACE TO A NATION DURING CRISIS.

BEING A LIGHT DOESN'T MEAN BEING PERFECT. IT MEANS CHOOSING KINDNESS, HONESTY, AND COURAGE IN THE LITTLE THINGS. WHEN PEOPLE SEE HOW YOU TREAT OTHERS WITH LOVE AND RESPECT, THEY'LL NOTICE SOMETHING DIFFERENT ABOUT YOU. THAT DIFFERENCE GIVES GOD GLORY.

JOSEPH DIDN'T HAVE A MICROPHONE OR A BIG STAGE, BUT HIS ACTIONS SPOKE LOUDLY. HE LIVED OUT GOD'S VALUES IN HIS WORK, AND THAT CREATED REAL CHANGE. YOUR ACTIONS MATTER TOO.

DAILY REFLECTION
Daily Reflection

Today,

WHERE HAS GOD PLACED YOU TO SHINE YOUR LIGHT?

_____
_____
_____
_____
_____
_____

Today,

WHAT DOES IT LOOK LIKE TO SERVE GOD IN YOUR JOB, SCHOOL, OR COMMUNITY?

_____
_____
_____
_____
_____
_____

Today,

WHAT IS ONE SMALL ACT OF KINDNESS YOU CAN DO TODAY?

_____
_____
_____
_____
_____

TAKE NOTICE OF SOMEONE IN YOUR LIFE WHO NEEDS ENCOURAGEMENT— SEND A KIND MESSAGE OR OFFER HELP.

_____
_____
_____
_____
_____
_____

BEGIN EACH DAY THIS WEEK BY ASKING GOD TO USE YOU AS A LIGHT WHEREVER YOU GO.

_____
_____
_____
_____
_____

MAKE A LIST OF WAYS YOU'VE SEEN OTHERS SHINE THEIR LIGHT— USE IT FOR INSPIRATION!

_____
_____
_____
_____
_____

OBEDIENCE TODAY PREPARES YOU FOR INFLUENCE TOMORROW.

SCRIPTURE MEDITATION

ARISE, SHINE; FOR YOUR LIGHT HAS COME! AND THE GLORY OF THE LORD IS RISEN UPON YOU."
—ISAIAH 60:1 (NKJV)

MEDITATION REFLECTION

GOD HAS PLACED HIS LIGHT WITHIN YOU TO SHINE IN EVERY PLACE YOU GO. JUST LIKE JOSEPH IN EGYPT, YOU ARE CALLED TO REFLECT GOD'S TRUTH AND LOVE IN DARK SPACES. DON'T HIDE YOUR LIGHT—LET IT BRING WARMTH, HOPE, AND CLARITY TO OTHERS.

KEY POINTS

- YOUR LIGHT REVEALS GOD'S LOVE.
- EVERYDAY CHOICES CAN GLORIFY GOD.
- FAITH-FILLED LEADERSHIP CHANGES ENVIRONMENTS.

DEAR GOD,
HELP ME TO SHINE YOUR LIGHT
IN MY EVERYDAY LIFE. TEACH
ME TO LEAD LIKE JOSEPH—
WITH WISDOM, LOVE, AND
HUMILITY. I WANT MY ACTIONS
TO REFLECT YOUR TRUTH AND
HOPE. USE MY WORK, WORDS,
AND HEART TO GLORIFY YOU IN
ALL I DO.
IN JESUS' NAME, AMEN.

JOURNAL REFLECTION-NEXT STEPS
Journal Reflection-Next Steps

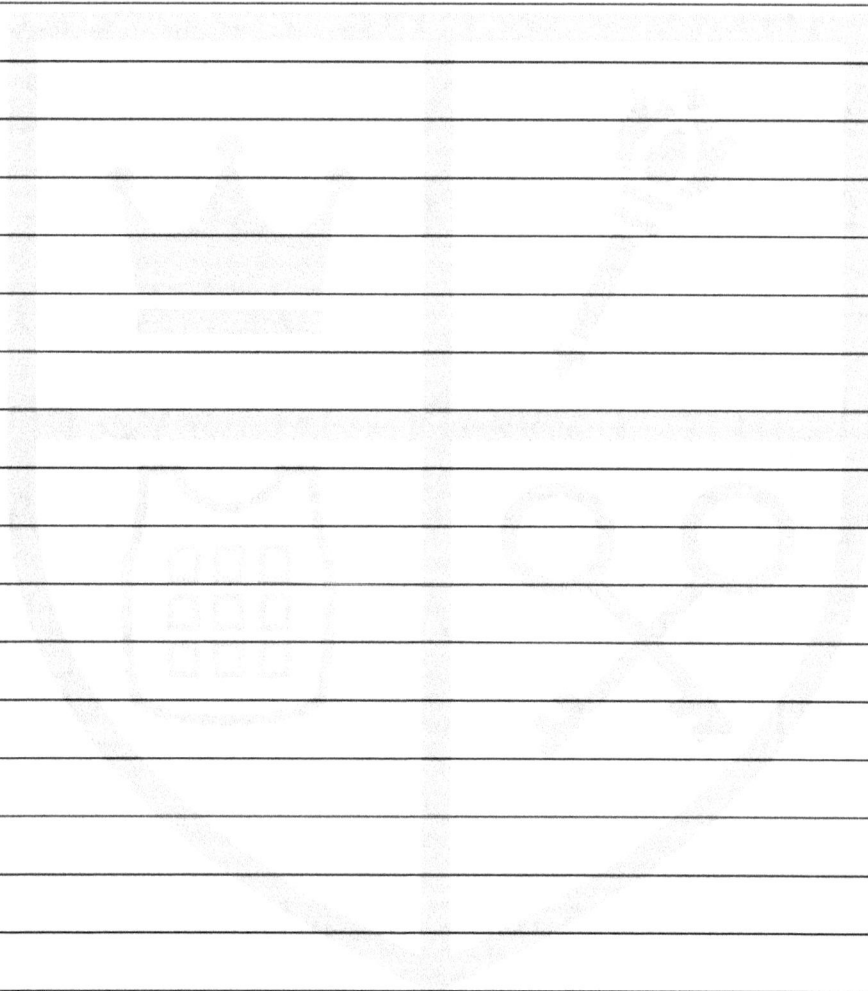

_____
_____
_____
_____
_____
_____
_____
_____
_____
_____
_____
_____
_____
_____
_____
_____
_____
_____
_____
_____
_____
_____
_____

"DO YOU SEE A MAN WHO EXCELS IN HIS WORK? HE WILL STAND BEFORE KINGS; HE WILL NOT STAND BEFORE UNKNOWN MEN."

–PROVERBS 22:29 (NKJV)

DEVOTIONAL READING

JOSEPH DIDN'T TRY TO BE FAMOUS OR POWERFUL. HE SIMPLY SERVED WITH EXCELLENCE, AND GOD OPENED DOORS FOR HIM TO STAND BEFORE KINGS. THAT'S HOW KINGDOM INFLUENCE WORKS. IT'S NOT ABOUT SHOWING OFF—IT'S ABOUT SHOWING UP WITH INTEGRITY, LOVE, AND EXCELLENCE.

EACH PART OF OUR SOCIETY—LIKE FAMILY, EDUCATION, BUSINESS, MEDIA, AND GOVERNMENT—IS CALLED A "PILLAR" OF CULTURE. GOD WANTS TO BRING HIS TRUTH INTO EVERY ONE OF THOSE PLACES. HE USES PEOPLE LIKE YOU TO DO IT. THAT MEANS YOUR CLASSROOM, JOB, OR HOME IS MORE THAN A PLACE—IT'S YOUR MISSION FIELD.

JOSEPH CHANGED EGYPT BY LIVING OUT HIS FAITH IN HIS WORK. HE FORGAVE OTHERS, MANAGED RESOURCES WISELY, AND TREATED PEOPLE FAIRLY. YOU CAN DO THE SAME BY BEING HONEST, HUMBLE, AND KIND. WHEN YOU LIVE WITH KINGDOM VALUES, PEOPLE SEE GOD IN YOU.

DAILY REFLECTION
Daily Reflection

Today,

WHICH OF THE SEVEN CULTURAL PILLARS (FAMILY, EDUCATION, GOVERNMENT, BUSINESS, MEDIA, ARTS, RELIGION) DO YOU FEEL DRAWN TO?

_____
_____
_____
_____
_____

Today,

HOW CAN YOU USE YOUR SKILLS AND INFLUENCE TO REFLECT GOD'S HEART?

_____
_____
_____
_____
_____

Today,

WHAT'S ONE THING YOU CAN DO TO BRING PEACE AND TRUTH INTO YOUR SPACE?

_____
_____
_____
_____
_____

WRITE DOWN THE PILLAR YOU FEEL CALLED TO INFLUENCE AND PRAY FOR DIRECTION IN THAT AREA.

_____
_____
_____
_____
_____
_____

LOOK FOR A SMALL WAY TO SHOW KINDNESS OR LEADERSHIP AT WORK, SCHOOL, OR HOME.

_____
_____
_____
_____
_____
_____

ASK GOD TO GIVE YOU WISDOM LIKE HE GAVE JOSEPH, SO YOU CAN LEAD WITH COURAGE AND GRACE.

_____
_____
_____
_____
_____
_____

WHEN GOD GIVES YOU A VISION, HE WILL ALSO GIVE YOU THE STRATEGY.

SCRIPTURE MEDITATION

"YOU ARE THE SALT OF THE EARTH; BUT IF THE SALT LOSES ITS FLAVOR, HOW SHALL IT BE SEASONED? IT IS THEN GOOD FOR NOTHING BUT TO BE THROWN OUT AND TRAMPLED UNDERFOOT BY MEN. YOU ARE THE LIGHT OF THE WORLD. A CITY THAT IS SET ON A HILL CANNOT BE HIDDEN."

–MATTHEW 5:13–14 (NKJV)

MEDITATION REFLECTION

GOD USES PEOPLE LIKE JOSEPH TO INFLUENCE CULTURE THROUGH VALUES, NOT VOLUME. BEING SALT MEANS PRESERVING TRUTH; BEING LIGHT MEANS GUIDING OTHERS TO HOPE. YOUR CHARACTER IN THE WORKPLACE, FAMILY, OR COMMUNITY IS A KINGDOM TOOL THAT TRANSFORMS ATMOSPHERES.

KEY POINTS

- INFLUENCE FLOWS FROM CHARACTER, NOT POSITION.
- GOD PLANTS YOU IN CULTURE TO REFLECT HIS VALUES.
- EXCELLENCE AND HUMILITY ATTRACT FAVOR.

HEAVENLY FATHER, THANK YOU FOR GIVING ME A PLACE IN YOUR BIGGER STORY. SHOW ME HOW TO USE MY INFLUENCE FOR GOOD AND LEAD WITH KINGDOM VALUES. HELP ME TO LOVE WELL, ACT JUSTLY, AND WALK HUMBLY WITH YOU. OPEN DOORS FOR ME TO REFLECT YOUR LIGHT IN EVERY AREA OF MY LIFE. IN JESUS' NAME, AMEN.

JOURNAL REFLECTION-NEXT STEPS
Journal Reflection-Next Steps

"NOW WHEN THEY SAW HIM AFAR OFF, EVEN BEFORE HE CAME NEAR THEM, THEY CONSPIRED AGAINST HIM TO KILL HIM... WE SHALL SEE WHAT WILL BECOME OF HIS DREAMS!"

– GENESIS 37:18–20 (NKJV)

GREAT LEADERSHIP DOESN'T BEGIN IN COMFORT—IT OFTEN STARTS IN CRISIS. JOSEPH'S LIFE CHANGED WHEN THOSE CLOSEST TO HIM BETRAYED HIM. BEING SOLD INTO SLAVERY BY HIS BROTHERS WAS MORE THAN PAINFUL—IT WAS THE BEGINNING OF A PROCESS GOD WOULD USE TO SHAPE HIS HEART. EVEN WHEN REJECTED AND ABANDONED, JOSEPH HELD ON TO WHAT GOD HAD SHOWN HIM.

GOD DOESN'T WASTE TRIALS. IN FACT, THEY OFTEN BECOME THE CLASSROOM WHERE HE BUILDS HUMILITY, WISDOM, AND ENDURANCE IN US. JOSEPH DIDN'T BECOME A LEADER OVERNIGHT. IT WAS THE LONG ROAD OF TESTING—IN POTIPHAR'S HOUSE, IN PRISON, AND THROUGH INJUSTICE—THAT MADE HIM READY. IN THE SAME WAY, YOUR HARDEST SEASONS MAY BE THE VERY GROUND WHERE GOD IS GROWING YOU INTO A TRUSTED, POWERFUL LEADER.

Today,

**WHAT PAIN OR
SETBACK IN YOUR LIFE
HAS TAUGHT YOU THE
MOST?**

_____
_____
_____
_____
_____
_____

Today,

**HOW DO YOU THINK
GOD IS SHAPING YOUR
CHARACTER IN THIS
SEASON?**

_____
_____
_____
_____
_____
_____

Today,

**WHAT MIGHT CHANGE
IF YOU VIEWED YOUR
CURRENT STRUGGLE
AS PREPARATION?**

_____
_____
_____
_____
_____
_____

RECOGNIZE THE TRIAL: WRITE DOWN A CHALLENGE YOU'RE CURRENTLY FACING AND WHAT EMOTIONS IT BRINGS UP.

_____
_____
_____
_____
_____

ASK FOR GOD'S PERSPECTIVE: PRAY AND ASK GOD WHAT HE'S TEACHING YOU THROUGH IT.

_____
_____
_____
_____
_____

STAY PRESENT: DECIDE TO SHOW UP WITH EXCELLENCE EVEN WHILE YOU'RE WAITING FOR BREAKTHROUGH.

_____
_____
_____
_____
_____

HUMILITY KEEPS YOUR HEART ALIGNED WITH HEAVEN.

SCRIPTURE MEDITATION

"BELOVED, DO NOT THINK IT STRANGE CONCERNING THE FIERY TRIAL WHICH IS TO TRY YOU, AS THOUGH SOME STRANGE THING HAPPENED TO YOU; BUT REJOICE TO THE EXTENT THAT YOU PARTAKE OF CHRIST'S SUFFERINGS, THAT WHEN HIS GLORY IS REVEALED, YOU MAY ALSO BE GLAD WITH EXCEEDING JOY."
—1 PETER 4:12–13 (NKJV)

MEDITATION REFLECTION

GOD USES FIERY TRIALS TO REFINE FUTURE LEADERS. JOSEPH'S HARDSHIPS WERE TOOLS TO SHARPEN HIS LEADERSHIP. DON'T DESPISE YOUR WILDERNESS—IT'S PROOF THAT GOD IS SHAPING YOU INTO SOMEONE WHO CAN CARRY RESPONSIBILITY WITH GRACE AND STRENGTH.

KEY POINTS

- TRIALS ARE CLASSROOMS FOR LEADERSHIP.
- PAIN CAN SHAPE PURPOSE.
- ENDURANCE PRODUCES LASTING GROWTH.

FATHER, THANK YOU FOR BEING WITH ME EVEN IN HARD TIMES. WHEN LIFE FEELS UNFAIR OR LONELY, HELP ME REMEMBER YOU ARE AT WORK BEHIND THE SCENES. SHAPE MY HEART, GROW MY FAITH, AND PREPARE ME FOR THE CALLING YOU'VE PLACED ON MY LIFE. I TRUST THAT YOU ARE USING EVERY CHALLENGE FOR GOOD.

IN JESUS' NAME, AMEN.

JOURNAL REFLECTION-NEXT STEPS

Journal Reflection-Next Steps

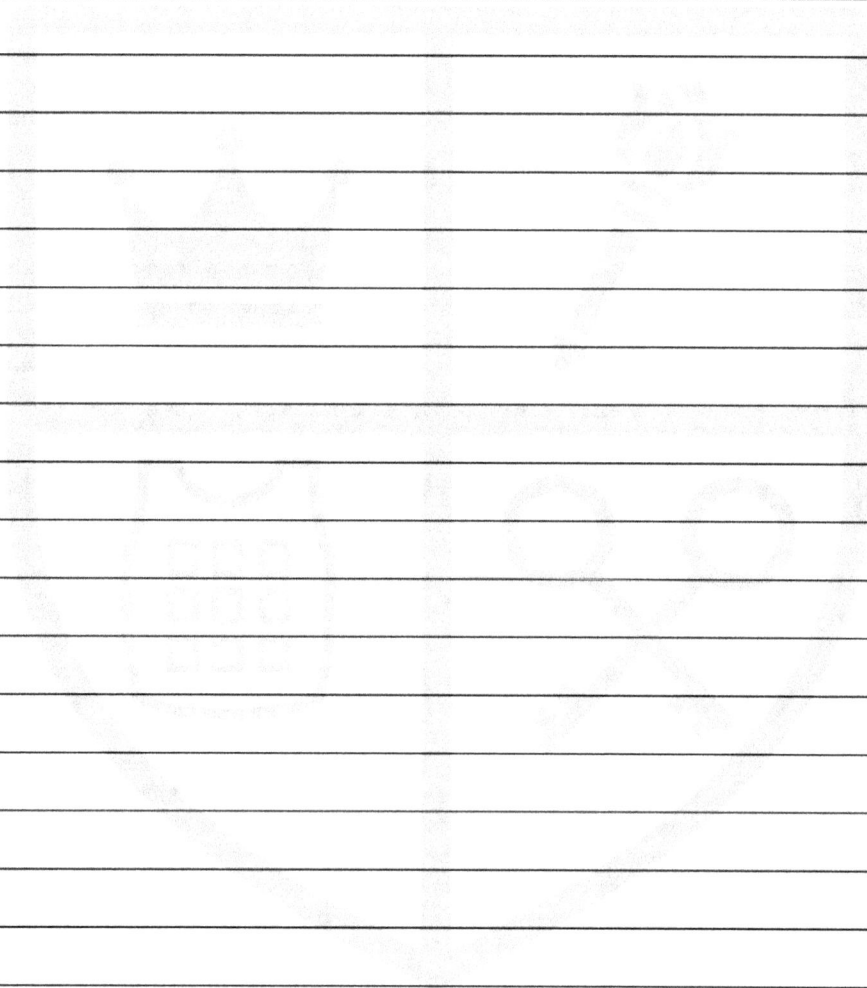

"BUT AS FOR YOU, YOU MEANT EVIL AGAINST ME; BUT GOD MEANT IT FOR GOOD, IN ORDER TO BRING IT ABOUT AS IT IS THIS DAY, TO SAVE MANY PEOPLE ALIVE."

– GENESIS 50:20 (NKJV)

JOSEPH DIDN'T JUST FACE BETRAYAL—HE ALSO HAD TO FORGIVE IT. THAT'S WHAT MADE HIM A POWERFUL LEADER. HE HAD EVERY RIGHT TO HOLD A GRUDGE AGAINST HIS BROTHERS AND POTIPHAR'S WIFE, BUT HE CHOSE TO TRUST GOD'S JUSTICE INSTEAD OF TAKING REVENGE. FORGIVENESS BECAME THE DOORWAY TO HIS FREEDOM AND INFLUENCE.

WHEN YOU HOLD ON TO BITTERNESS, IT CLOUDS YOUR JUDGMENT AND DRAINS YOUR ENERGY. BUT WHEN YOU FORGIVE, YOU RELEASE THAT WEIGHT AND MAKE SPACE FOR GOD'S PEACE TO TAKE OVER. AS JOSEPH SHOWED, FORGIVENESS IS NOT WEAKNESS—IT'S STRENGTH. IT'S A KINGDOM CHOICE THAT SAYS, "I TRUST GOD MORE THAN I TRUST MY OWN ANGER." THIS IS HOW GOD REFINES LEADERS—NOT JUST BY WHAT WE DO, BUT BY HOW WE LOVE.

DAILY REFLECTION
Daily Reflection

Today,

IS THERE SOMEONE YOU NEED TO FORGIVE SO YOU CAN MOVE FORWARD?

_____
_____
_____
_____
_____
_____

Today,

HOW HAS UNFORGIVENESS AFFECTED YOUR PEACE OR PURPOSE?

_____
_____
_____
_____
_____
_____

Today,

WHAT DOES IT LOOK LIKE TO LEAD WITH BOTH TRUTH AND GRACE?

_____
_____
_____
_____
_____

IDENTIFY THE WOUND: WRITE DOWN A HURT THAT STILL AFFECTS YOUR HEART.

_____
_____
_____
_____
_____
_____

FORGIVE WITH INTENTION: CHOOSE TO RELEASE THAT PAIN AND GIVE IT TO GOD TODAY.

_____
_____
_____
_____
_____
_____

PRACTICE GRACE: FIND A WAY TO SHOW KINDNESS THIS WEEK TO SOMEONE DIFFICULT OR DISTANT.

_____
_____
_____
_____
_____
_____

WAITING SEASONS ARE NEVER WASTED SEASONS.

SCRIPTURE MEDITATION

"CREATE IN ME A CLEAN HEART, O GOD, AND RENEW A STEADFAST SPIRIT WITHIN ME."
—PSALM 51:10 (NKJV)

MEDITATION REFLECTION

FORGIVENESS SOFTENS THE HEART AND STRENGTHENS YOUR LEADERSHIP. JOSEPH'S ABILITY TO FORGIVE HIS BROTHERS UNLOCKED HEALING FOR GENERATIONS. CHOOSING TO RELEASE BITTERNESS INVITES GOD TO FILL YOUR HEART WITH PEACE, CLARITY, AND RENEWED STRENGTH FOR YOUR CALLING.

KEY POINTS

- FORGIVENESS FREES YOU TO LEAD WELL.
- GOD REFINES HEARTS BEFORE RAISING LEADERS.
- BITTERNESS BLOCKS THE FLOW OF PURPOSE.

LORD,
THANK YOU FOR SHOWING ME
THAT LEADERSHIP STARTS IN
THE HEART. HELP ME FORGIVE
THOSE WHO HAVE HURT ME.
CLEAN OUT THE BITTERNESS,
THE FEAR, AND THE PAIN, AND
FILL ME WITH YOUR LOVE. I
WANT TO LEAD WITH PEACE,
WISDOM, AND STRENGTH.
REFINE ME UNTIL I LOOK MORE
LIKE YOU.
IN JESUS' NAME, AMEN.

JOURNAL REFLECTION-NEXT STEPS
Journal Reflection-Next Steps

"WAIT ON THE LORD; BE OF GOOD COURAGE, AND HE SHALL STRENGTHEN YOUR HEART; WAIT, I SAY, ON THE LORD!"

–PSALM 27:14 (NKJV)

DEVOTIONAL READING

BEFORE JOSEPH LED EGYPT, HE SPENT MANY YEARS IN DIFFICULT AND HIDDEN PLACES. THESE YEARS WERE NOT PUNISHMENT—THEY WERE PREPARATION. JOSEPH WENT THROUGH BETRAYAL, SLAVERY, AND PRISON, BUT GOD NEVER LEFT HIM. EVEN WHEN LIFE SEEMED UNFAIR, JOSEPH STAYED FAITHFUL.

THERE ARE TIMES WHEN WE FEEL INVISIBLE OR UNIMPORTANT. BUT JUST LIKE A SEED BURIED IN THE GROUND, WE ARE GROWING WHERE NO ONE ELSE CAN SEE. THESE QUIET SEASONS BUILD TRUST, HUMILITY, AND STRENGTH IN US. GOD IS DOING SOMETHING DEEP INSIDE YOU.

JESUS SAID IN JOHN 12:24-26 THAT A SEED MUST BE BURIED BEFORE IT GROWS AND MULTIPLIES. GOD HONORS THOSE WHO SERVE QUIETLY AND FAITHFULLY. JOSEPH'S HIDDEN YEARS MADE HIM READY FOR PUBLIC LEADERSHIP, AND THE SAME IS TRUE FOR YOU. YOUR HIDDEN SEASON IS SHAPING YOU FOR SOMETHING GREATER.

DAILY REFLECTION
Daily Reflection

Today,

ARE YOU IN A SEASON OF QUIET OR WAITING? HOW MIGHT GOD BE USING THIS TIME TO GROW YOU?

_____
_____
_____
_____
_____
_____
_____

Today,

HOW HAS GOD BEEN SHAPING YOUR CHARACTER, PATIENCE, OR FAITH IN THIS HIDDEN SEASON?

_____
_____
_____
_____
_____
_____
_____

Today,

ARE THERE AREAS WHERE YOU'VE BEEN RESISTING STILLNESS INSTEAD OF TRUSTING GOD'S TIMING?

_____
_____
_____
_____
_____
_____

PRAY FOR CLARITY: ASK GOD TO SHOW YOU WHAT HE IS BUILDING IN YOU DURING THIS SEASON.

_____
_____
_____
_____
_____
_____

RECOGNIZE GROWTH: WRITE DOWN ONE WAY GOD IS GROWING YOU —LIKE IN PATIENCE OR FAITH.

_____
_____
_____
_____
_____

EMBRACE STILLNESS: SET ASIDE QUIET TIME DAILY TO LISTEN, PRAY, OR REFLECT WITHOUT DISTRACTION.

_____
_____
_____
_____
_____

GOD SEES YOUR EFFORT, EVEN WHEN OTHERS DON'T.

MEDITATION SCRIPTURE

"BUT THOSE WHO WAIT ON THE LORD SHALL RENEW THEIR STRENGTH; THEY SHALL MOUNT UP WITH WINGS LIKE EAGLES, THEY SHALL RUN AND NOT BE WEARY, THEY SHALL WALK AND NOT FAINT."
–ISAIAH 40:31 (NKJV)

MEDITATION REFLECTION

WAITING SEASONS FEEL SLOW, BUT THEY ARE FULL OF PURPOSE. JOSEPH DIDN'T WASTE HIS HIDDEN YEARS—HE TRUSTED GOD AND GREW THROUGH THEM. ISAIAH 40:31 REMINDS US THAT THOSE WHO WAIT ON THE LORD FIND STRENGTH, ENDURANCE, AND HOPE. GOD MAY BE BUILDING SOMETHING IN YOU, EVEN IF NO ONE SEES IT YET. THESE HIDDEN MOMENTS MATTER. THEY PREPARE YOU TO WALK INTO YOUR CALLING WITH WISDOM AND FAITH. DON'T RUSH THE PROCESS—REST IN GOD'S TIMING AND BELIEVE THAT YOUR ROOTS ARE GROWING DEEPER IN HIM.

KEY POINTS

- HIDDEN SEASONS ARE FOR GROWTH AND DEEP PREPARATION.
- STILLNESS IS NOT A DELAY—IT'S PART OF GOD'S DESIGN.
- FAITHFULNESS IN QUIET PLACES LEADS TO FRUITFULNESS LATER.

DEAR GOD,
THANK YOU FOR THIS QUIET SEASON. EVEN WHEN I FEEL UNSEEN, I TRUST THAT YOU ARE SHAPING MY HEART AND PREPARING ME FOR MORE. HELP ME REMAIN FAITHFUL, HUMBLE, AND FULL OF TRUST.
GIVE ME STRENGTH WHEN I GROW TIRED AND HELP ME SEE THIS SEASON THE WAY YOU DO. I SURRENDER TO YOUR TIMELINE AND ASK YOU TO GROW ME IN EVERY WAY.
IN JESUS' NAME, AMEN.

JOURNAL REFLECTION-NEXT STEPS
Journal Reflection-Next Steps

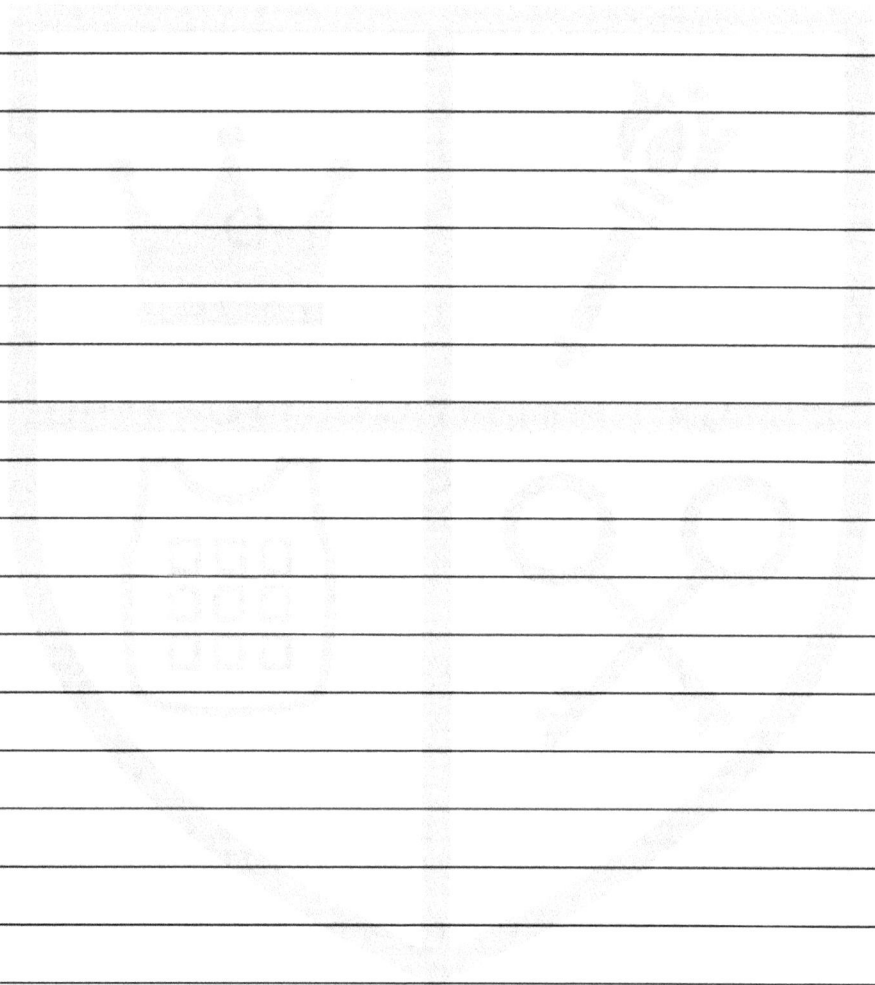

"BUT THE LORD WAS WITH JOSEPH AND SHOWED HIM MERCY, AND HE GAVE HIM FAVOR IN THE SIGHT OF THE KEEPER OF THE PRISON... WHATEVER HE DID, THE LORD MADE IT PROSPER."

–GENESIS 39:21–23 (NKJV)

EVEN WHEN JOSEPH WAS IN PRISON, HE STAYED FAITHFUL. HE DIDN'T BECOME BITTER—HE SERVED OTHERS WITH EXCELLENCE AND HONOR. HIS QUIET OBEDIENCE BECAME THE PATH TO HIS PROMOTION. GOD NOTICED, EVEN WHEN OTHERS DIDN'T.

GOD SEES WHAT YOU DO IN SECRET. HE REWARDS QUIET INTEGRITY, PATIENCE, AND SERVICE. LIKE JOSEPH, YOUR SMALL ACTS OF FAITHFULNESS MATTER MORE THAN YOU KNOW. THEY ARE PREPARING YOU FOR SOMETHING BIGGER.

LUKE 16:10 TELLS US THAT WHEN WE'RE FAITHFUL IN LITTLE THINGS, WE CAN BE TRUSTED WITH MORE. DON'T OVERLOOK THE POWER OF DAILY OBEDIENCE. KEEP SHOWING UP, WORKING HARD, AND TRUSTING GOD WITH THE RESULTS.

DAILY REFLECTION
Daily Reflection

Today,

WHAT SMALL TASK ARE YOU BEING ASKED TO DO WITH EXCELLENCE RIGHT NOW?

_____
_____
_____
_____
_____
_____

Today,

HAVE YOU BEEN TEMPTED TO GIVE UP BECAUSE YOUR FAITHFULNESS FEELS UNNOTICED?

_____
_____
_____
_____
_____
_____

Today,

HOW CAN YOU REMIND YOURSELF THAT GOD SEES AND HONORS THE WORK YOU DO IN SECRET?

_____
_____
_____
_____
_____
_____

EXAMINE YOUR ATTITUDE: ASK GOD TO HELP YOU SERVE WITH JOY, EVEN IN SMALL ROLES.

_____
_____
_____
_____
_____
_____

SERVE WHERE YOU ARE: CHOOSE ONE WAY TO BE FAITHFUL IN YOUR CURRENT SEASON OR JOB.

_____
_____
_____
_____
_____
_____

LOOK FOR GOD'S FAVOR: WRITE DOWN A MOMENT THIS WEEK WHERE YOU SAW GOD BLESS YOUR FAITHFULNESS.

_____
_____
_____
_____
_____
_____

SPEAK LIFE OVER YOUR DREAMS —YOUR WORDS CARRY POWER.

SCRIPTURE MEDITATION

"AND LET US NOT GROW WEARY WHILE DOING GOOD, FOR IN DUE SEASON WE SHALL REAP IF WE DO NOT LOSE HEART."
—GALATIANS 6:9 (NKJV)

MEDITATION REFLECTION

FAITHFULNESS BEHIND THE SCENES IS NOT WASTED. GOD OFTEN TESTS OUR CHARACTER IN QUIET PLACES BEFORE OPENING DOORS IN PUBLIC PLACES. JOSEPH'S TIME IN PRISON PROVED THAT GOD'S FAVOR CAN REST ON US EVEN IN HARD CIRCUMSTANCES. KEEP DOING WHAT'S RIGHT, EVEN WHEN IT'S HARD. YOUR DILIGENCE IS TRAINING YOU FOR MORE RESPONSIBILITY. IN DUE TIME, YOUR FAITHFULNESS WILL BEAR FRUIT—JUST LIKE IT DID FOR JOSEPH.

KEY POINTS

- GOD SEES YOUR BEHIND-THE-SCENES OBEDIENCE AND HONORS IT.
- PROMOTION OFTEN COMES AFTER LONG SEASONS OF FAITHFULNESS.
- DO YOUR BEST NOW, AND TRUST GOD WITH WHAT'S NEXT.

HEAVENLY FATHER,
THANK YOU FOR SEEING EVERY
EFFORT I MAKE, EVEN WHEN
OTHERS DO NOT. HELP ME SERVE
WITH JOY AND STAY FAITHFUL,
EVEN WHEN THE SEASON FEELS
QUIET OR SMALL. TEACH ME TO
WORK WITH EXCELLENCE AND
TRUST YOU FOR INCREASE.
I BELIEVE YOU ARE USING THIS
TIME TO SHAPE MY HEART AND
MY FUTURE. MAY EVERYTHING I
DO BRING YOU GLORY.
IN JESUS' NAME, AMEN.

"SO JOSEPH FOUND FAVOR IN HIS SIGHT, AND SERVED HIM. THEN HE MADE HIM OVERSEER OF HIS HOUSE, AND ALL THAT HE HAD HE PUT UNDER HIS AUTHORITY... THE LORD BLESSED THE EGYPTIAN'S HOUSE FOR JOSEPH'S SAKE."

–GENESIS 39:4–5 (NKJV)

DEVOTIONAL READING

JOSEPH DIDN'T START IN THE PALACE—HE STARTED IN SOMEONE ELSE'S HOUSE. BEFORE GOD GAVE HIM LEADERSHIP OVER A NATION, JOSEPH PROVED HIMSELF FAITHFUL IN EVERYDAY SERVICE. HE DIDN'T WAIT FOR A TITLE TO START GIVING HIS BEST. HE HONORED GOD WITH HIS WORK, EVEN WHEN LIFE WAS HARD AND UNFAIR.

GOD OFTEN PREPARES US IN PLACES WHERE NO ONE ELSE IS LOOKING. WHEN WE SERVE WITH INTEGRITY IN THE QUIET PLACES, WE SHOW THAT WE CAN BE TRUSTED WITH MORE. JOSEPH'S EXAMPLE REMINDS US THAT LEADERSHIP IN GOD'S KINGDOM DOESN'T COME FROM STRIVING—IT COMES FROM SERVING.

THERE IS NO TASK TOO SMALL TO MATTER TO GOD. WHEN YOU HELP SOMEONE, CLEAN UP, LEAD WITH KINDNESS, OR GIVE YOUR BEST IN SMALL THINGS, YOU ARE BUILDING THE CHARACTER OF A TRUE LEADER. FAITHFULNESS IN THE SMALL THINGS BECOMES THE TRAINING GROUND FOR GREATER THINGS AHEAD.

Today,

**WHERE IN YOUR LIFE
ARE YOU BEING ASKED
TO SERVE FAITHFULLY
RIGHT NOW?**

_____
_____
_____
_____
_____
_____

Today,

**HOW IS GOD SHAPING
YOUR CHARACTER
THROUGH THE SMALL
THINGS?**

_____
_____
_____
_____
_____
_____

Today,

**WHAT DO YOU THINK IT
MEANS TO SERVE "AS
UNTO THE LORD"?**

_____
_____
_____
_____
_____
_____

PRACTICE EXCELLENCE: CHOOSE ONE TASK THIS WEEK AND DO IT TO THE BEST OF YOUR ABILITY—NO SHORTCUTS, NO GRUMBLING.

_____
_____
_____
_____
_____
_____

WRITE A GRATITUDE LIST: LIST FIVE SMALL THINGS YOU'RE GRATEFUL FOR IN YOUR CURRENT SEASON OF SERVING.

_____
_____
_____
_____
_____

PRAY FOR HUMILITY: ASK GOD TO HELP YOU SEE SERVICE AS HONOR, NOT BURDEN.

_____
_____
_____
_____
_____

FAVOR FOLLOWS FAITHFULNESS.

SCRIPTURE MEDITATION

"DO YOU SEE A MAN WHO EXCELS IN HIS WORK? HE WILL STAND BEFORE KINGS; HE WILL NOT STAND BEFORE UNKNOWN MEN."
– PROVERBS 22:29 (NKJV)

MEDITATION REFLECTION

JOSEPH'S EXCELLENCE IN SERVICE DIDN'T BEGIN IN PHARAOH'S PALACE—IT STARTED IN POTIPHAR'S HOUSE AND THE PRISON CELL. HE CHOSE TO SERVE WITH DILIGENCE, HONOR, AND FAITHFULNESS, EVEN IN PLACES THAT SEEMED SMALL OR HIDDEN. HIS COMMITMENT TO EXCELLENCE POSITIONED HIM FOR PROMOTION WHEN THE TIME WAS RIGHT. THIS SCRIPTURE REMINDS US THAT EXCELLENCE ISN'T OPTIONAL FOR KINGDOM LEADERS—IT'S A DISTINGUISHING MARK. YOU DON'T HAVE TO SEEK RECOGNITION OR STRIVE FOR PROMOTION. IF YOU SERVE FAITHFULLY WHERE YOU ARE, GOD WILL OPEN DOORS IN HIS PERFECT TIMING. EXCELLENCE DRAWS ATTENTION—NOT FOR APPLAUSE, BUT FOR KINGDOM INFLUENCE. WHETHER YOU'RE IN A HIGH-LEVEL POSITION OR WORKING BEHIND THE SCENES, DO YOUR WORK WITH EXCELLENCE AS UNTO THE LORD. PROMOTION IN THE KINGDOM COMES TO THOSE WHO STEWARD WELL WHAT THEY'VE BEEN GIVEN—EVEN WHEN NO ONE IS WATCHING.

KEY POINTS

- EXCELLENCE PRECEDES PROMOTION: BEFORE JOSEPH LED A NATION, HE LED WITH EXCELLENCE IN PRISON. GOD WATCHES HOW YOU HANDLE THE SMALL THINGS.
- FAITHFUL SERVICE HONORS GOD: DOING YOUR BEST—EVEN WHEN IT'S UNNOTICED—SHOWS SPIRITUAL MATURITY AND POSITIONS YOU FOR GREATER INFLUENCE.
- PROMOTION COMES FROM THE LORD: KINGDOM ADVANCEMENT IS NOT ABOUT STRIVING BUT ABOUT STEWARDSHIP AND FAITHFULNESS.

FATHER,
THANK YOU FOR THE PRIVILEGE
OF SERVING OTHERS. TEACH ME
TO LEAD THROUGH SUPPORT, TO
SERVE WITH GLADNESS, AND TO
GROW THROUGH HUMILITY. USE
THIS SEASON TO SHARPEN MY
PERSPECTIVE, STRETCH MY
CAPACITY, AND PREPARE ME FOR
MY OWN ASSIGNMENT. LET ME BE
FAITHFUL IN SMALL THINGS SO I
MAY BE ENTRUSTED WITH
GREATER.
IN JESUS' NAME, AMEN.

JOURNAL REFLECTION-NEXT STEPS
Journal Reflection-Next Steps

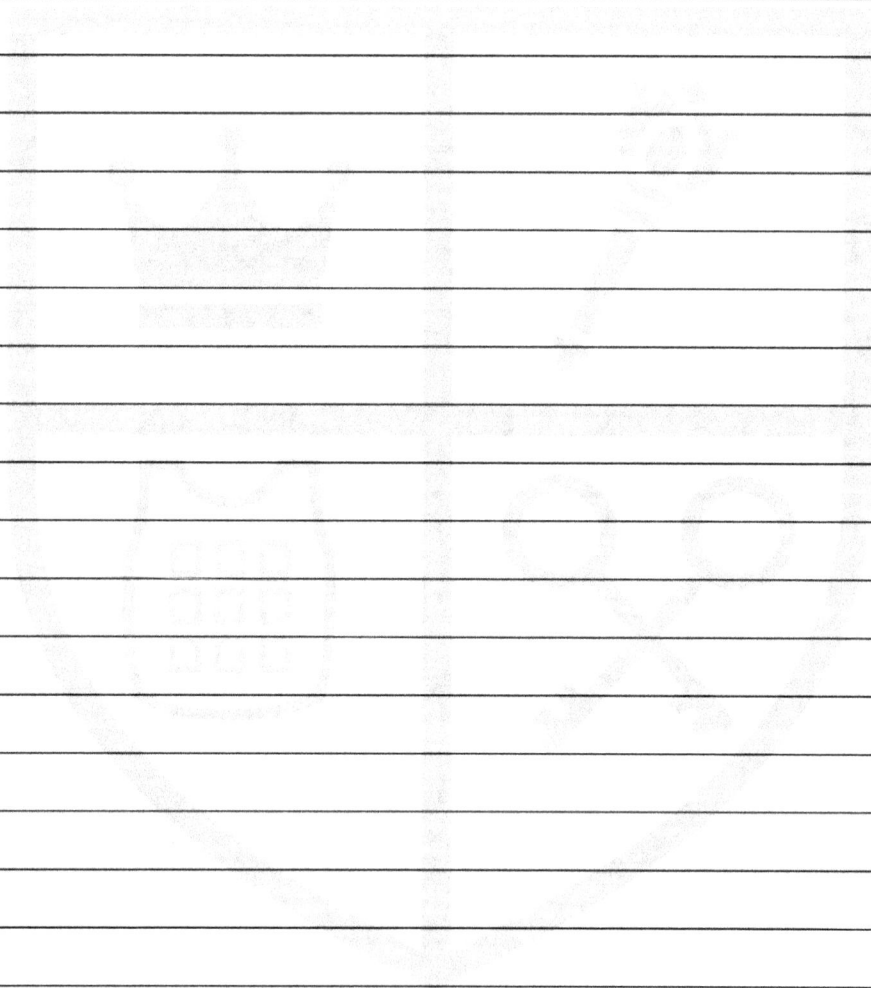

"DO NOT DESPISE THESE SMALL BEGINNINGS, FOR THE LORD REJOICES TO SEE THE WORK BEGIN..."

—ZECHARIAH 4:10 (NLT)

DEVOTIONAL READING

SOMETIMES IT FEELS LIKE WHAT WE'RE DOING DOESN'T MATTER. IT MAY BE HIDDEN, THANKLESS, OR UNNOTICED BY OTHERS. BUT SCRIPTURE TELLS US THAT GOD REJOICES IN THE BEGINNING—EVEN THE SMALL, SLOW, ORDINARY ONES. JOSEPH'S STORY PROVES THAT FAITHFUL SERVICE IN QUIET PLACES LEADS TO LEADERSHIP IN PUBLIC PLACES.

WHILE IN PRISON AND AS A SLAVE, JOSEPH WORKED WITH EXCELLENCE. HE WASN'T LOOKING FOR APPLAUSE. HE SIMPLY HONORED GOD WITH HIS EFFORT AND ATTITUDE. THIS CONSISTENCY REVEALED HIS CHARACTER, AND GOD USED THOSE SEASONS TO PREPARE HIM FOR GREATER INFLUENCE.

WHATEVER SEASON YOU'RE IN NOW, KNOW THIS: IT MATTERS. YOUR FAITHFULNESS IN YOUR HOME, JOB, SCHOOL, OR MINISTRY IS NOT OVERLOOKED. GOD SEES, AND HE IS USING EVERY SMALL ACT TO PREPARE YOU FOR WHAT'S COMING. STEWARD THE SMALL THINGS WELL—THEY ARE THE BUILDING BLOCKS OF YOUR FUTURE.

Today,

**WHAT AREA OF YOUR
LIFE NEEDS MORE
FAITHFULNESS OR
FOCUS?**

_____
_____
_____
_____
_____
_____

Today,

**ARE THERE PLACES
WHERE YOU'VE BEEN
TEMPTED TO GIVE LESS
THAN YOUR BEST?**

_____
_____
_____
_____
_____

Today,

**WHAT COULD IT LOOK
LIKE TO SERVE
JOYFULLY IN THIS
SEASON?**

_____
_____
_____
_____
_____

CHOOSE FAITHFULNESS: PICK ONE "SMALL THING" YOU OFTEN OVERLOOK AND CHOOSE TO GIVE YOUR FULL HEART TO IT TODAY.

_____
_____
_____
_____
_____
_____

REMEMBER A PAST VICTORY: REFLECT ON A TIME WHEN GOD USED A SMALL STEP TO OPEN A BIG DOOR.

_____
_____
_____
_____
_____
_____

ENCOURAGE SOMEONE: SPEAK LIFE OVER SOMEONE ELSE'S SMALL BEGINNING. YOUR ENCOURAGEMENT COULD HELP THEM KEEP GOING.

_____
_____
_____
_____
_____

EVEN IN HARD PLACES, YOU CAN GROW.

SCRIPTURE MEDITATION

"WHATEVER YOU DO, DO IT HEARTILY, AS TO THE LORD AND NOT TO MEN."
–COLOSSIANS 3:23 (NKJV)

MEDITATION REFLECTION

WHEN YOU DO YOUR BEST BEHIND THE SCENES, YOU'RE HONORING GOD. JOSEPH DIDN'T LOOK FOR APPLAUSE–HE LOOKED FOR OPPORTUNITIES TO SERVE. THAT'S WHY GOD COULD TRUST HIM WITH MORE. THE SAME IS TRUE FOR YOU. YOUR QUIET OBEDIENCE IS PREPARING YOU FOR SOMETHING GREATER. DON'T RUSH IT. STAY CONSISTENT, STAY HUMBLE, AND LET GOD SHAPE YOUR FUTURE ONE STEP AT A TIME.

KEY POINTS

- FAITHFULNESS STARTS SMALL: GOD WATCHES HOW WE HANDLE WHAT'S IN FRONT OF US.
- SERVING BUILDS TRUST: JOSEPH EARNED LEADERSHIP THROUGH HUMILITY AND HARD WORK.
- GOD HONORS CONSISTENCY: EVERY FAITHFUL ACT IS A SEED FOR YOUR FUTURE.

DEAR GOD,
THANK YOU FOR SEEING THE VALUE IN EVERY SMALL ACT OF SERVICE. HELP ME TO STAY FAITHFUL EVEN WHEN NO ONE ELSE NOTICES. TEACH ME TO SERVE WITH JOY, HUMILITY, AND EXCELLENCE. SHAPE ME INTO A LEADER WHO HONORS YOU IN EVERY SEASON.
IN JESUS' NAME, AMEN.

"THE INTEGRITY OF THE UPRIGHT WILL GUIDE THEM, BUT THE PERVERSITY OF THE UNFAITHFUL WILL DESTROY THEM."
–PROVERBS 11:3 (NKJV)

DEVOTIONAL READING

TRUE LEADERSHIP ISN'T BUILT OVERNIGHT. IT'S SHAPED IN MOMENTS WHEN NO ONE IS WATCHING. JOSEPH WAS TESTED WITH TEMPTATION, LIES, AND REJECTION—BUT THROUGH IT ALL, HE CHOSE INTEGRITY. HE STAYED FAITHFUL TO GOD'S TRUTH EVEN WHEN IT COST HIM EVERYTHING.

INTEGRITY MEANS DOING WHAT'S RIGHT WHEN IT'S NOT POPULAR OR EASY. JOSEPH DIDN'T COMPROMISE, EVEN WHEN IT WOULD'VE MADE HIS LIFE MORE COMFORTABLE. HE SAID NO TO POTIPHAR'S WIFE, KNOWING TROUBLE MIGHT FOLLOW— BUT HE CHOSE TO HONOR GOD. THAT KIND OF STRENGTH COMES FROM A DEEP COMMITMENT TO TRUTH.

YOU MAY BE FACING PRESSURE TO GIVE IN, GO ALONG, OR STAY QUIET WHEN YOU KNOW SOMETHING IS WRONG. BUT REMEMBER: GOD SEES YOUR DECISIONS. HE REWARDS THOSE WHO WALK IN INTEGRITY. YOUR FAITHFULNESS NOW IS SHAPING THE LEADER YOU'RE BECOMING.

DAILY REFLECTION
Daily Reflection

Today,

WHAT SITUATION ARE YOU FACING THAT REQUIRES YOU TO STAND STRONG IN INTEGRITY?

_____
_____
_____
_____
_____
_____

Today,

HOW DOES JOSEPH'S EXAMPLE ENCOURAGE YOU TO DO THE RIGHT THING, EVEN WHEN IT'S HARD?

_____
_____
_____
_____
_____
_____

Today,

WHERE IN YOUR LIFE DO YOU NEED TO ASK GOD FOR STRENGTH TO WALK UPRIGHTLY?

_____
_____
_____
_____
_____
_____

WHERE IN YOUR LIFE DO YOU NEED TO ASK GOD FOR STRENGTH TO WALK UPRIGHTLY?

_____
_____
_____
_____
_____
_____

SEEK ACCOUNTABILITY: TALK WITH A TRUSTED FRIEND OR MENTOR ABOUT THE AREAS YOU WANT TO GROW IN INTEGRITY.

_____
_____
_____
_____
_____

PRAY FOR COURAGE: ASK GOD TO GIVE YOU BOLDNESS TO CHOOSE WHAT HONORS HIM.

_____
_____
_____
_____
_____

WALK IN EXCELLENCE, NOT PERFECTION.

SCRIPTURE MEDITATION

"WHOEVER WALKS IN INTEGRITY WALKS SECURELY, BUT WHOEVER TAKES CROOKED PATHS WILL BE FOUND OUT."
—PROVERBS 10:9 (NIV)

MEDITATION REFLECTION

INTEGRITY GIVES YOU PEACE AND STRENGTH. WHEN YOUR LIFE LINES UP WITH YOUR VALUES, YOU DON'T HAVE TO LIVE IN FEAR OR REGRET. JOSEPH DIDN'T KNOW WHAT WOULD HAPPEN NEXT, BUT HE TRUSTED GOD MORE THAN HIS CIRCUMSTANCES.

YOUR INTEGRITY IS YOUR GUIDE. IT'S NOT ABOUT BEING PERFECT—IT'S ABOUT BEING HONEST, FAITHFUL, AND CONSISTENT. GOD BLESSES THOSE WHO WALK IN TRUTH. KEEP YOUR HEART PURE AND YOUR STEPS FIRM. EVEN IN THE SHADOWS, GOD IS WORKING THROUGH YOUR OBEDIENCE.

KEY POINTS

- INTEGRITY PROTECTS AND GUIDES YOU.
- GOD REWARDS FAITHFUL CHOICES.
- CHARACTER IS PROVEN IN THE HARD MOMENTS.

DEAR GOD,
HELP ME WALK WITH INTEGRITY EVERY DAY. STRENGTHEN ME WHEN I FACE PRESSURE TO GIVE IN OR HIDE THE TRUTH. TEACH ME TO STAND FOR WHAT IS RIGHT, NO MATTER THE COST. LET MY ACTIONS REFLECT YOUR HEART AND HELP OTHERS TRUST YOU THROUGH MY EXAMPLE.
IN JESUS' NAME, AMEN.

JOURNAL REFLECTION-NEXT STEPS

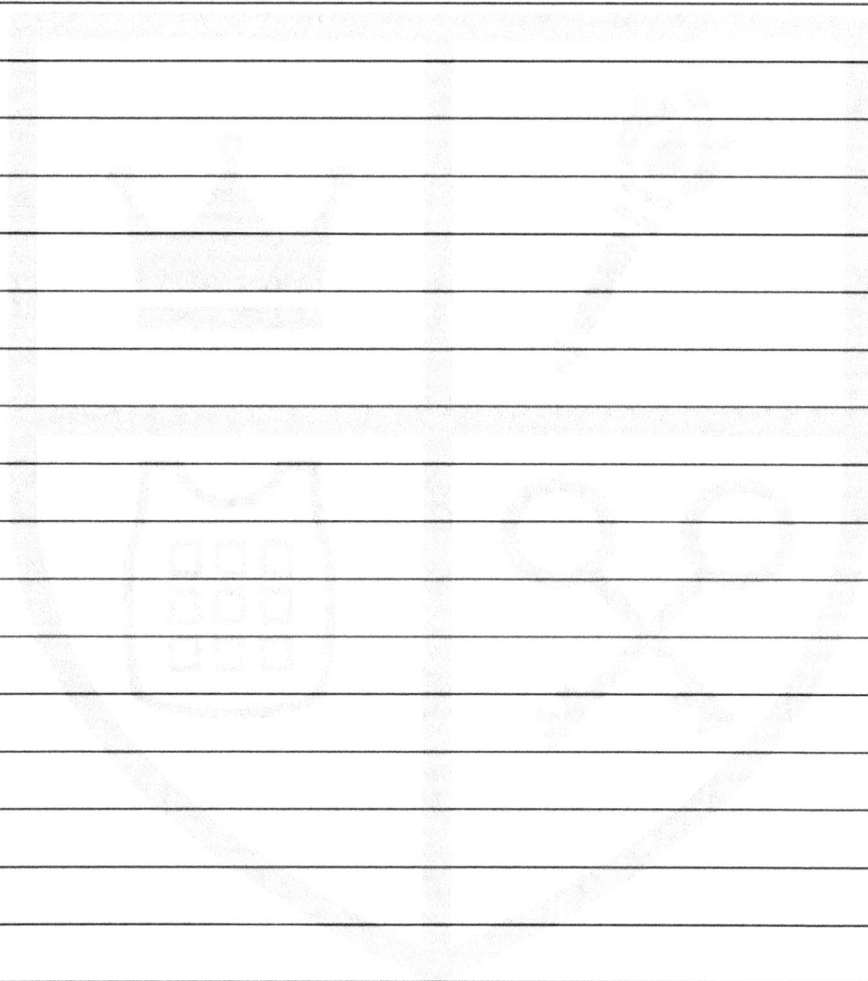

"AND NOT ONLY THAT, BUT WE ALSO GLORY IN TRIBULATIONS, KNOWING THAT TRIBULATION PRODUCES PERSEVERANCE; AND PERSEVERANCE, CHARACTER; AND CHARACTER, HOPE."

–ROMANS 5:3–4 (NKJV)

JOSEPH DIDN'T RISE TO LEADERSHIP BECAUSE HE WAS LUCKY. HE GOT THERE BECAUSE HE STAYED FAITHFUL IN DIFFICULTY. BETRAYED BY HIS BROTHERS, LIED ABOUT BY POTIPHAR'S WIFE, AND FORGOTTEN IN PRISON—JOSEPH HAD EVERY REASON TO GIVE UP. BUT HE DIDN'T. HE ALLOWED TRIALS TO SHAPE HIS CHARACTER.

WHEN WE FACE PRESSURE, OUR CHOICES MATTER EVEN MORE. THAT'S WHEN OUR CHARACTER IS TESTED AND GROWN. JOSEPH CHOSE TO FORGIVE, TO SERVE, AND TO TRUST GOD NO MATTER WHAT. HIS STRENGTH DIDN'T COME FROM POSITION—IT CAME FROM WHO HE WAS WHEN NO ONE WAS LOOKING.

REAL LEADERSHIP ISN'T ABOUT TALENT OR TITLES—IT'S ABOUT CHARACTER. GOD WANTS TO BUILD SOMETHING STRONG IN YOU THAT CAN'T BE SHAKEN. THAT STRENGTH COMES FROM TRUSTING HIM IN THE STORM, STANDING FIRM IN TRUTH, AND CHOOSING TO HONOR HIM IN EVERYTHING YOU DO.

DAILY REFLECTION
Daily Reflection

Today,

HOW HAVE YOUR PAST TRIALS SHAPED YOUR CHARACTER AND FAITH?

_____
_____
_____
_____
_____
_____

Today,

ARE YOU ALLOWING CHALLENGES TO BUILD YOU OR BREAK YOU?

_____
_____
_____
_____
_____
_____

Today,

WHAT PART OF JOSEPH'S STORY REMINDS YOU TO TRUST GOD DURING HARD SEASONS?

_____
_____
_____
_____

REFLECT ON GROWTH: WRITE ABOUT A HARD TIME THAT HELPED YOU GROW IN PERSEVERANCE OR PATIENCE.

_____
_____
_____
_____
_____
_____
_____

SERVE ANYWAY: LIKE JOSEPH, SERVE SOMEONE THIS WEEK EVEN IF YOU'RE IN YOUR OWN HARD SEASON.

_____
_____
_____
_____
_____
_____

SPEAK LIFE: ENCOURAGE SOMEONE WHO'S GOING THROUGH A CHALLENGE RIGHT NOW.

_____
_____
_____
_____
_____
_____

THE LORD PROMOTES THOSE WHO SERVE WITH INTEGRITY.

SCRIPTURE MEDITATION

"HE WHO IS FAITHFUL IN WHAT IS LEAST IS FAITHFUL ALSO IN MUCH."
—LUKE 16:10 (NKJV)

MEDITATION REFLECTION

CHARACTER SHOWS UP IN THE QUIET PLACES. JOSEPH DIDN'T WAIT FOR A TITLE TO START LIVING LIKE A LEADER—HE SERVED WITH EXCELLENCE IN A PRISON CELL. HE DIDN'T LET BITTERNESS WIN. HE CHOSE FAITHFULNESS.

THAT SAME CHOICE IS IN FRONT OF YOU. WILL YOU HONOR GOD IN THE SMALL THINGS? WILL YOU SHOW KINDNESS WHEN IT'S HARD AND STAY FAITHFUL WHEN IT'S NOT FAIR? GOD SEES IT ALL, AND HE IS PREPARING YOU FOR SOMETHING GREATER.

KEY POINTS

- LEADERSHIP STARTS IN PRIVATE BEFORE IT'S SEEN IN PUBLIC.
- TRIALS GROW PERSEVERANCE, AND PERSEVERANCE BUILDS STRONG CHARACTER.
- FAITHFULNESS IN THE SMALL THINGS PREPARES YOU FOR THE BIG ONES.

DEAR GOD,
THANK YOU FOR USING EVERY
SEASON—ESPECIALLY THE
HARD ONES—TO SHAPE ME.
WHEN I FEEL TIRED, HELP ME
KEEP SHOWING UP WITH
FAITH. BUILD IN ME A HEART OF
INTEGRITY, HUMILITY, AND
STRENGTH. LET MY LIFE
REFLECT YOUR TRUTH AND
LOVE, EVEN WHEN NO ONE IS
WATCHING.
IN JESUS' NAME, AMEN.

JOURNAL REFLECTION-NEXT STEPS
Journal Reflection-Next Steps

DAY 15: WAITING WITH PURPOSE

"AND YOU SHALL REMEMBER THAT THE LORD YOUR GOD LED YOU ALL THE WAY THESE FORTY YEARS IN THE WILDERNESS, TO HUMBLE YOU AND TEST YOU, TO KNOW WHAT WAS IN YOUR HEART, WHETHER YOU WOULD KEEP HIS COMMANDMENTS OR NOT. SO HE HUMBLED YOU, ALLOWED YOU TO HUNGER, AND FED YOU WITH MANNA WHICH YOU DID NOT KNOW NOR DID YOUR FATHERS KNOW, THAT HE MIGHT MAKE YOU KNOW THAT MAN SHALL NOT LIVE BY BREAD ALONE; BUT MAN LIVES BY EVERY WORD THAT PROCEEDS FROM THE MOUTH OF THE LORD."

—DEUTERONOMY 8:2–3 (NKJV)

DEVOTIONAL READING

WAITING CAN FEEL REALLY HARD. SOMETIMES IT SEEMS LIKE NOTHING IS HAPPENING AND EVERYONE HAS FORGOTTEN YOU. BUT IN GOD'S KINGDOM, WAITING ISN'T WASTED— IT'S A TIME OF PREPARATION. GOD OFTEN USES QUIET AND HIDDEN SEASONS TO GROW OUR FAITH, SHAPE OUR HEARTS, AND GET US READY FOR SOMETHING GREATER.

JOSEPH'S TIME IN PRISON WAS A LONG SEASON OF WAITING. PEOPLE MAY HAVE FORGOTTEN HIM, BUT GOD NEVER DID. WHILE IT SEEMED LIKE LIFE HAD PAUSED, JOSEPH STAYED FAITHFUL TO WHAT WAS IN FRONT OF HIM. HE KEPT SERVING OTHERS AND USING HIS GIFTS, TRUSTING THAT GOD HAD NOT FORGOTTEN HIS DREAMS.

HARD SEASONS ARE OFTEN WHERE WE GROW THE MOST. IT MIGHT FEEL LIKE NOTHING IS CHANGING ON THE OUTSIDE, BUT INSIDE, GOD IS BUILDING STRENGTH AND MATURITY. LIKE ROOTS GROWING UNDERGROUND, WE'RE BEING MADE STRONGER FOR WHAT'S COMING. EVEN THOUGH WE DON'T ENJOY THE HARD MOMENTS, THEY'RE IMPORTANT. GOD IS PREPARING US FOR FUTURE RESPONSIBILITY.

Today.

WHAT IS GOD TEACHING YOU DURING YOUR CURRENT SEASON OF WAITING?

_____
_____
_____
_____
_____
_____

Today.

WHAT IS GOD TEACHING YOU DURING YOUR CURRENT SEASON OF WAITING?

_____
_____
_____
_____
_____
_____

Today.

HOW CAN YOU USE YOUR GIFTS RIGHT NOW TO SERVE OTHERS, EVEN IF NO ONE SEES IT?

_____
_____
_____
_____
_____
_____

GROW WHERE YOU ARE: CHOOSE ONE AREA—LIKE YOUR SKILLS, SPIRITUAL LIFE, OR RELATIONSHIPS—TO DEVELOP WHILE YOU WAIT.

_____
_____
_____
_____
_____
_____

USE YOUR GIFTS QUIETLY: FIND A WAY TO SERVE OTHERS WITH YOUR TALENTS, EVEN IN SMALL OR BEHIND-THE-SCENES WAYS.

_____
_____
_____
_____
_____

TRUST THE PROCESS: WHEN YOU FEEL FRUSTRATED OR TIRED, REMIND YOURSELF THAT GOD'S TIMING IS PERFECT.

_____
_____
_____
_____
_____

KEEP YOUR HEART SOFT, EVEN IN TOUGH SITUATIONS.

SCRIPTURE MEDITATION

"BUT THOSE WHO WAIT ON THE LORD SHALL RENEW THEIR STRENGTH; THEY SHALL MOUNT UP WITH WINGS LIKE EAGLES, THEY SHALL RUN AND NOT BE WEARY, THEY SHALL WALK AND NOT FAINT."
—ISAIAH 40:31 (NKJV)

MEDITATION REFLECTION

WAITING CAN BE HARD. IT'S EASY TO FEEL LIKE NOTHING IS HAPPENING OR THAT YOUR TIME IS BEING WASTED. BUT IN GOD'S KINGDOM, WAITING SEASONS ARE FULL OF PURPOSE. WHILE JOSEPH WAS WAITING, GOD WAS SHAPING HIS HEART, BUILDING HIS CHARACTER, AND TRAINING HIM TO LEAD. YOUR WAITING SEASON IS NOT A DELAY—IT'S DEVELOPMENT. GOD MAY BE TEACHING YOU PATIENCE, BUILDING RESILIENCE, OR SHOWING YOU HOW TO TRUST HIM MORE DEEPLY. WAITING ISN'T SITTING AROUND—IT'S STAYING FAITHFUL AND TRUSTING GOD TO WORK IT ALL OUT IN HIS TIME.

KEY POINTS

- WAITING IS PART OF YOUR PREPARATION.
- YOUR FAITHFULNESS TODAY IS BUILDING YOUR FUTURE.
- GOD NEVER FORGETS WHAT HE PROMISED.

DEAR GOD,
THANK YOU FOR USING THIS WAITING SEASON TO SHAPE ME. HELP ME SEE IT NOT AS A PAUSE BUT AS A TIME TO GROW STRONGER, WISER, AND MORE FAITHFUL. GIVE ME PATIENCE AND HELP ME STAY FAITHFUL, EVEN WHEN NO ONE SEES. I BELIEVE YOU ARE PREPARING ME FOR SOMETHING GREATER.
IN JESUS' NAME, AMEN.

JOURNAL REFLECTION-NEXT STEPS
Journal Reflection-Next Steps

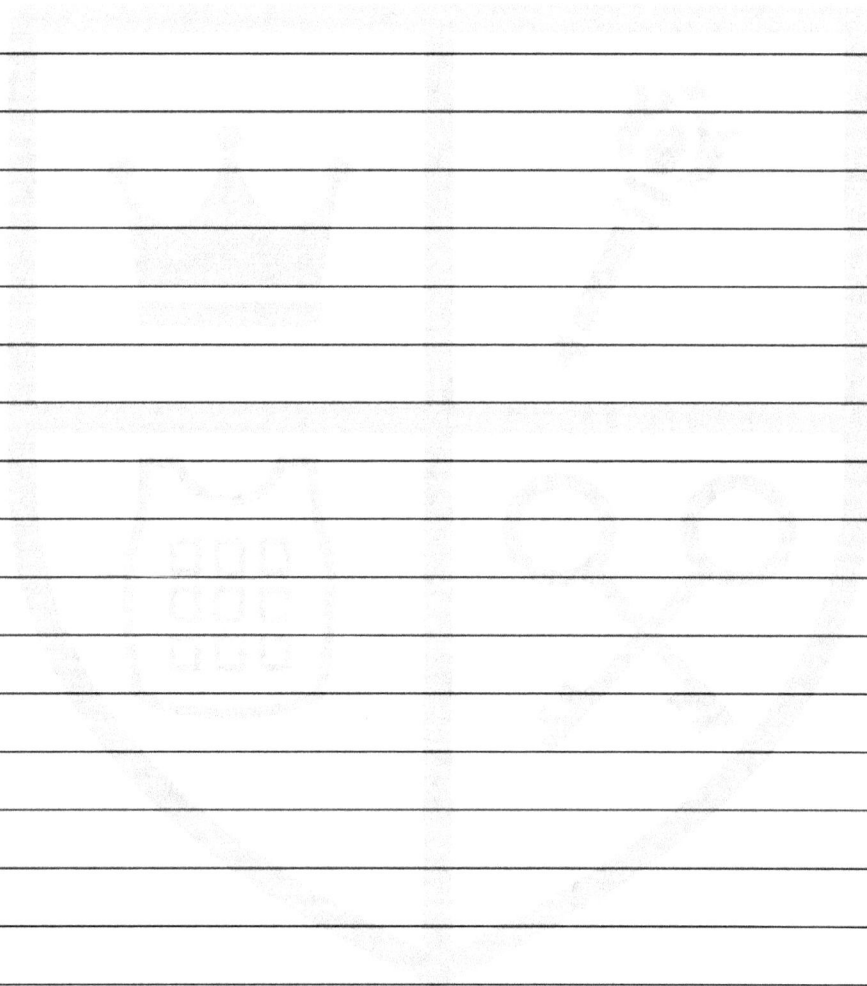

DAY 16: FAITHFUL IN HIDDEN PLACES

"FOR YOU, O GOD, HAVE TESTED US; YOU HAVE REFINED US AS SILVER IS REFINED."

–PSALM 66:10 (NKJV)

DEVOTIONAL READING

JOSEPH HAD EVERY REASON TO BE DISCOURAGED. HE HELPED THE KING'S BUTLER IN PRISON, BUT WHEN THE BUTLER GOT OUT, "THE CHIEF BUTLER DID NOT REMEMBER JOSEPH BUT FORGOT HIM." (GENESIS 40:23) THAT MUST HAVE HURT DEEPLY. STILL, JOSEPH STAYED COMMITTED AND DIDN'T GIVE UP.

HARD SEASONS ARE WHERE WE LEARN TO LEAN ON GOD. HE IS STRENGTHENING YOU BEHIND THE SCENES. GOD USED JOSEPH'S TIME IN PRISON TO BUILD THE MATURITY AND HUMILITY HE WOULD NEED AS A LEADER. JUST LIKE JOSEPH, OUR GROWTH OFTEN HAPPENS IN PLACES WHERE WE FEEL UNSEEN.

JOSEPH'S TIME IN PRISON WASN'T A DELAY—IT WAS PART OF GOD'S DESIGN. IT'S NOT ABOUT HOW FAST WE GET TO OUR DREAM—IT'S ABOUT HOW READY WE ARE WHEN THE DOOR OPENS. THAT'S WHY THE WILDERNESS IS A TRAINING GROUND. GOD PREPARES OUR HEARTS SO WE CAN CARRY THE WEIGHT OF OUR CALLING WELL.

DAILY REFLECTION
Daily Reflection

Today,

**HAVE YOU EVER FELT
FORGOTTEN LIKE
JOSEPH? HOW DID YOU
RESPOND?**

_____
_____
_____
_____
_____
_____

Today,

**WHAT HAS GOD
TAUGHT YOU DURING
YOUR "HIDDEN"
SEASONS?**

_____
_____
_____
_____
_____
_____

Today,

**HOW CAN YOU STAY
FAITHFUL WHEN
RECOGNITION IS
MISSING?**

_____
_____
_____
_____
_____

SERVE IN SECRET: THIS WEEK, DO SOMETHING KIND WITHOUT EXPECTING ATTENTION OR THANKS.

_____
_____
_____
_____
_____
_____
_____

JOURNAL THE JOURNEY: WRITE ABOUT A SEASON WHEN GOD GREW YOUR FAITH QUIETLY.

_____
_____
_____
_____
_____

PRAY FOR ENDURANCE: ASK GOD FOR STRENGTH TO REMAIN FAITHFUL WHERE YOU ARE.

_____
_____
_____
_____
_____

DON'T RUSH THE PROCESS—GOD IS DOING SOMETHING DEEP.

SCRIPTURE MEDITATION

"HE WHO IS FAITHFUL IN WHAT IS LEAST IS FAITHFUL ALSO IN MUCH."
—LUKE 16:10 (NKJV)

MEDITATION REFLECTION

BEING FAITHFUL IN SMALL PLACES IS A POWERFUL PART OF LEADERSHIP. JOSEPH DIDN'T WAIT FOR A SPOTLIGHT—HE SERVED IN THE SHADOWS. IN PRISON, HE HELPED OTHERS, INTERPRETED DREAMS, AND GAVE HIS BEST EVEN WHEN FORGOTTEN.

YOUR HIDDEN SEASON IS NOT WASTED. IT'S WHERE CHARACTER IS BUILT, MOTIVES ARE PURIFIED, AND YOUR HEART BECOMES STRONG ENOUGH TO CARRY GOD'S CALL. STAY STEADY. KEEP SERVING. TRUST THAT GOD IS PREPARING YOU FOR THE NEXT STEP.

KEY POINTS

- GOD SEES YOUR HIDDEN FAITHFULNESS.
- GROWTH OFTEN HAPPENS IN QUIET PLACES.
- EVERY MOMENT OF OBEDIENCE BUILDS SPIRITUAL STRENGTH.

DEAR GOD,
THANK YOU FOR SEEING ME IN THE HIDDEN PLACES. WHEN I FEEL FORGOTTEN OR UNSEEN, HELP ME REMEMBER YOU ARE WATCHING. TEACH ME TO SERVE WITH JOY AND TRUST YOU WITH THE OUTCOME. LET THIS SEASON GROW MY FAITH, SHAPE MY HEART, AND PREPARE ME FOR MORE.
IN JESUS' NAME, AMEN.

"A MAN'S GIFT MAKES ROOM FOR HIM, AND BRINGS HIM BEFORE GREAT MEN."

—PROVERBS 18:16 (NKJV)

DEVOTIONAL READING

WHEN GOD OPENS A DOOR, WE NEED TO BE READY TO WALK THROUGH IT. BUT THAT KIND OF READINESS DOESN'T HAPPEN OVERNIGHT. JOSEPH DIDN'T GO FROM PRISON TO THE PALACE IN ONE DAY. HE SPENT YEARS LEARNING, GROWING, AND PREPARING IN QUIET PLACES SO HE COULD STEP INTO LEADERSHIP WHEN THE TIME WAS RIGHT.

GOD OFTEN BEGINS PREPARING US BEFORE WE EVEN KNOW WHAT HE'S PREPARING US FOR. JOSEPH DIDN'T WASTE HIS TIME IN SLAVERY OR PRISON. HE LEARNED HOW TO MANAGE PEOPLE, SOLVE PROBLEMS, AND STAY FAITHFUL IN PRESSURE-FILLED PLACES. SO WHEN PHARAOH NEEDED SOMEONE WISE AND TRUSTWORTHY, JOSEPH WAS READY.

PROVERBS 3:5–6 SAYS, "TRUST IN THE LORD WITH ALL YOUR HEART, AND LEAN NOT ON YOUR OWN UNDERSTANDING; IN ALL YOUR WAYS ACKNOWLEDGE HIM, AND HE SHALL DIRECT YOUR PATHS." GOD'S PREPARATION OFTEN FEELS HIDDEN, BUT IT'S NEVER WASTED. EVEN IF OTHERS DON'T NOTICE, GOD IS SHAPING YOU FOR THE DOORS HE'S GOING TO OPEN.

Today,

HOW CAN YOU PREPARE NOW FOR THE OPPORTUNITIES GOD MAY BRING IN THE FUTURE?

_____
_____
_____
_____
_____
_____

Today,

ARE THERE SKILLS OR HABITS YOU NEED TO GROW WHILE WAITING FOR GOD'S TIMING?

_____
_____
_____
_____
_____
_____

Today,

WHAT DOES IT LOOK LIKE TO STAY FAITHFUL AND DILIGENT IN THE SEASON YOU'RE IN RIGHT NOW?

_____
_____
_____
_____
_____
_____

STRENGTHEN ONE AREA: CHOOSE ONE PART OF YOUR LIFE— LIKE PRAYER, LEADERSHIP, OR TIME MANAGEMENT—TO GROW IN THIS WEEK.

_____
_____
_____
_____
_____

PRAY FOR DISCERNMENT: ASK GOD TO HELP YOU NOTICE DIVINE OPPORTUNITIES AND GIVE YOU THE COURAGE TO WALK THROUGH THE RIGHT DOORS.

_____
_____
_____
_____

STAY FAITHFUL NOW: KEEP GIVING YOUR BEST TO THE ROLES AND RESPONSIBILITIES YOU ALREADY HAVE, TRUSTING THAT THEY'RE PART OF YOUR PREPARATION.

_____
_____
_____
_____

FORGIVENESS FREES YOUR FUTURE.

SCRIPTURE MEDITATION

"I KNOW YOUR WORKS. SEE, I HAVE SET BEFORE YOU AN OPEN DOOR, AND NO ONE CAN SHUT IT; FOR YOU HAVE A LITTLE STRENGTH, HAVE KEPT MY WORD, AND HAVE NOT DENIED MY NAME."
—REVELATION 3:8 (NKJV)

MEDITATION REFLECTION

GOD IS THE ONE WHO OPENS DOORS—AND WHEN HE OPENS ONE, NO ONE CAN SHUT IT. THAT'S A POWERFUL TRUTH. EVEN WHEN YOU FEEL SMALL OR UNQUALIFIED, GOD KNOWS YOUR HEART AND YOUR FAITHFULNESS. HE'S NOT LOOKING FOR PERFECTION—HE'S LOOKING FOR READINESS.

JOSEPH'S STORY REMINDS US THAT BIG MOMENTS OFTEN FOLLOW SEASONS OF QUIET PREPARATION. BEFORE STANDING BEFORE PHARAOH, JOSEPH SERVED FAITHFULLY IN POTIPHAR'S HOUSE AND PRISON. HE DIDN'T KNOW WHEN HIS OPPORTUNITY WOULD COME, BUT HE STAYED READY. WHEN THE TIME CAME, HE STEPPED UP WITH WISDOM AND COURAGE.

KEY POINTS

- GOD OPENS DOORS IN HIS TIMING.
- PREPARATION BUILDS READINESS.
- YOUR SEASON RIGHT NOW MATTERS.

DEAR GOD,
THANK YOU FOR EVERY SEASON OF PREPARATION. HELP ME TRUST THAT YOU ARE LEADING ME, EVEN WHEN I DON'T SEE EVERYTHING CLEARLY. GROW MY HEART TO BE FAITHFUL, FOCUSED, AND READY FOR THE DOORS YOU WILL OPEN. I SURRENDER MY TIMELINE AND TRUST YOUR PLAN. USE ME FOR YOUR GLORY.
IN JESUS' NAME, AMEN.

JOURNAL REFLECTION-NEXT STEPS
Journal Reflection-Next Steps

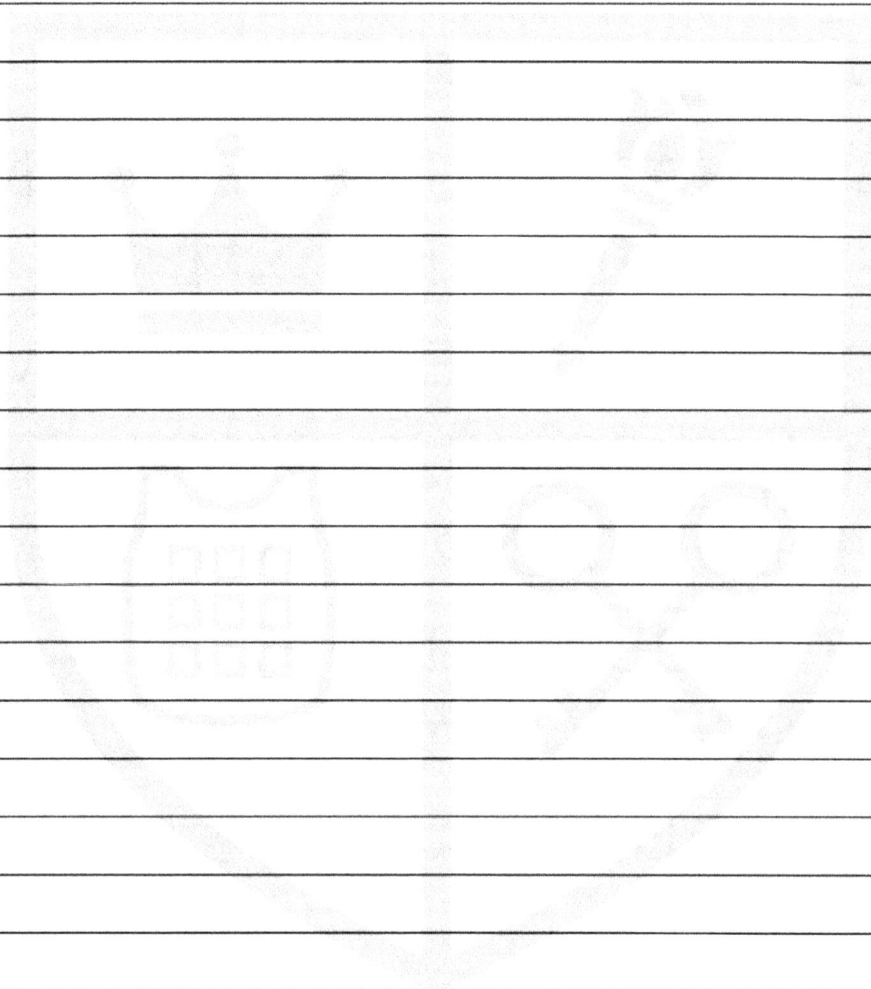

_____
_____
_____
_____
_____
_____
_____
_____
_____
_____
_____
_____
_____
_____
_____
_____
_____
_____
_____
_____
_____
_____

"LET THIS MIND BE IN YOU WHICH WAS ALSO IN CHRIST JESUS."

–PHILIPPIANS 2:5 (NKJV)

DEVOTIONAL READING

JOSEPH USED HIS INFLUENCE TO SERVE OTHERS, NOT HIMSELF. HE DIDN'T BECOME ARROGANT WITH POWER OR SEEK REVENGE. INSTEAD, HE USED HIS POSITION TO HELP PEOPLE, SAVE LIVES, AND RESTORE RELATIONSHIPS. THAT'S WHAT A KINGDOM MINDSET LOOKS LIKE IN ACTION.

JESUS LIVED TO SERVE AND LOVE, EVEN WHEN IT WAS HARD. HE DIDN'T CLIMB THE RANKS FOR FAME—HE GAVE HIS LIFE FOR OTHERS. MARK 10:45 SAYS, "FOR EVEN THE SON OF MAN DID NOT COME TO BE SERVED, BUT TO SERVE, AND TO GIVE HIS LIFE A RANSOM FOR MANY." WHEN WE LEAD WITH HIS MINDSET, OUR DECISIONS LOOK DIFFERENT. WE CHOOSE COMPASSION, HUMILITY, AND JUSTICE OVER PRIDE.

YOUR GIFTS WERE NEVER JUST FOR YOUR SUCCESS—THEY WERE MEANT TO BLESS OTHERS. WHEN YOU LEAD WITH A KINGDOM HEART, YOU POINT PEOPLE TO JESUS. GOD OPENS DOORS FOR THOSE WHO ARE READY TO LEAD WITH LOVE. STAYING HUMBLE AND WILLING MAKES YOU A LEADER WHO LASTS.

DAILY REFLECTION
Daily Reflection

Today,

WHAT DOES A KINGDOM MINDSET LOOK LIKE IN YOUR LIFE?

_____
_____
_____
_____
_____
_____

Today,

ARE THERE AREAS WHERE PRIDE, FEAR, OR CONTROL NEED TO BE REPLACED WITH HUMILITY AND TRUST?

_____
_____
_____
_____
_____
_____

Today,

HOW CAN YOU USE YOUR LEADERSHIP OR INFLUENCE TO SERVE OTHERS THIS WEEK?

_____
_____
_____
_____
_____
_____

SERVE SOMEONE: CHOOSE A WAY TO BLESS SOMEONE AROUND YOU USING YOUR TIME, GIFTS, OR ATTENTION.

_____
_____
_____
_____
_____
_____

CHECK YOUR MOTIVES: ASK YOURSELF IF YOU'RE LEADING FOR GOD'S GLORY OR PERSONAL GAIN. INVITE GOD TO REALIGN YOUR HEART.

_____
_____
_____
_____
_____

PRACTICE HUMILITY: THIS WEEK, LET SOMEONE ELSE GO FIRST, GIVE CREDIT AWAY, OR DO A TASK WITHOUT NEEDING THANKS.

_____
_____
_____
_____
_____

STAY PLANTED—GOD WILL PRODUCE FRUIT IN DUE SEASON.

SCRIPTURE MEDITATION

"HE WHO FOLLOWS RIGHTEOUSNESS AND MERCY FINDS LIFE, RIGHTEOUSNESS, AND HONOR."
—PROVERBS 21:21 (NKJV)

MEDITATION REFLECTION

KINGDOM LEADERSHIP ISN'T ABOUT MAKING YOURSELF LOOK GOOD—IT'S ABOUT MAKING GOD KNOWN. JOSEPH DIDN'T ASK FOR POWER, BUT HE RECEIVED IT BECAUSE HE SERVED WITH HUMILITY AND WISDOM. HE STAYED FAITHFUL IN SMALL PLACES, AND WHEN THE TIME CAME, HE GAVE GLORY TO GOD.

INFLUENCE IS A GIFT. WHEN USED WITH A KINGDOM MINDSET, IT CHANGES LIVES, BUILDS TRUST, AND HONORS GOD. YOU DON'T HAVE TO FORCE YOUR WAY FORWARD—JUST STAY FAITHFUL. LET GOD GUIDE YOUR STEPS AND SHAPE YOUR HEART TO LEAD LIKE JESUS.

KEY POINTS

- A KINGDOM MINDSET PUTS GOD FIRST.
- INFLUENCE IS FOR SERVICE, NOT SELF-PROMOTION.
- LEADING LIKE JESUS BRINGS LASTING IMPACT.

DEAR GOD,
THANK YOU FOR EVERY OPPORTUNITY TO LEAD AND SERVE. HELP ME TO LEAD WITH HUMILITY, LOVE, AND WISDOM. TEACH ME TO KEEP MY HEART FOCUSED ON YOU AND TO SERVE OTHERS WITH JOY. LET MY LIFE POINT PEOPLE TO YOUR KINGDOM. IN JESUS' NAME, AMEN.

JOURNAL REFLECTION-NEXT STEPS
Journal Reflection-Next Steps

"AND YOU SHALL REMEMBER THE LORD YOUR GOD, FOR IT IS HE WHO GIVES YOU POWER TO GET WEALTH, THAT HE MAY ESTABLISH HIS COVENANT WHICH HE SWORE TO YOUR FATHERS, AS IT IS THIS DAY."

–DEUTERONOMY 8:18 (NKJV)

DEVOTIONAL READING

BEING AN ENTREPRENEUR TAKES MORE THAN GOOD IDEAS OR WANTING TO MAKE MONEY. TRUE KINGDOM ENTREPRENEURSHIP BEGINS WITH PURPOSE. IT'S ABOUT USING YOUR GIFTS TO SOLVE PROBLEMS, BLESS OTHERS, AND BRING GLORY TO GOD. JOSEPH'S STORY REMINDS US THAT SUCCESS COMES FROM LEADING WITH BOTH VISION AND FAITH.

PROVERBS 21:5 REMINDS US, "THE PLANS OF THE DILIGENT LEAD SURELY TO PLENTY, BUT THOSE OF EVERYONE WHO IS HASTY, SURELY TO POVERTY." JOSEPH DIDN'T JUST SAVE EGYPT—HE CREATED SYSTEMS THAT HELPED NATIONS SURVIVE. HE LED WITH WISDOM, VISION, AND STRATEGY. THAT KIND OF IMPACT STARTS WITH A HEART THAT LISTENS TO GOD AND OBEYS.

WHEN GOD GIVES YOU A DREAM, IT MIGHT SEEM IMPOSSIBLE. BUT AS JESUS SAID IN MATTHEW 19:26, "WITH MEN THIS IS IMPOSSIBLE, BUT WITH GOD ALL THINGS ARE POSSIBLE." TRUST THAT IF GOD GAVE YOU THE VISION, HE'LL GIVE YOU WHAT YOU NEED TO WALK IT OUT.

Today,

HOW CAN YOU USE YOUR BUSINESS OR LEADERSHIP ROLE TO REFLECT KINGDOM VALUES?

_____
_____
_____
_____
_____
_____

Today,

WHAT IS ONE AREA OF YOUR BUSINESS WHERE YOU NEED TO TRUST GOD'S TIMING AND GUIDANCE?

_____
_____
_____
_____
_____
_____

Today,

HOW CAN YOU HELP BUILD A CULTURE OF HONESTY, GENEROSITY, AND SERVANT LEADERSHIP IN YOUR WORKPLACE?

_____
_____
_____
_____
_____

LIVE YOUR VALUES: CHOOSE ONE WAY TO PRACTICE KINGDOM PRINCIPLES IN YOUR DAILY BUSINESS DECISIONS—LIKE SHOWING HONESTY, GENEROSITY, OR GRACE.

_____
_____
_____
_____
_____
_____

BLESS SOMEONE THROUGH BUSINESS: IDENTIFY ONE PERSON OR GROUP TO SUPPORT THROUGH YOUR TIME, RESOURCES, OR INFLUENCE THIS WEEK.

_____
_____
_____
_____
_____

PRAY OVER YOUR WORK: SET TIME ASIDE TO PRAY OVER YOUR BUSINESS OR CAREER, ASKING GOD TO LEAD YOU WITH WISDOM AND OPEN THE RIGHT DOORS.

_____
_____
_____
_____
_____

LEAD WITH COMPASSION, NOT CONTROL.

SCRIPTURE MEDITATION

"AND YOU SHALL REMEMBER THE LORD YOUR GOD, FOR IT IS HE WHO GIVES YOU POWER TO GET WEALTH, THAT HE MAY ESTABLISH HIS COVENANT..."
–DEUTERONOMY 8:18 (NKJV)

MEDITATION REFLECTION

YOUR BUSINESS OR INFLUENCE ISN'T JUST ABOUT MONEY–IT'S ABOUT IMPACT. JOSEPH SERVED WITH EXCELLENCE, MANAGED WISELY, AND STAYED FAITHFUL. HE DIDN'T USE HIS POSITION FOR SELFISH GAIN. INSTEAD, HE BECAME A BLESSING TO MANY.

DEUTERONOMY 8:18 REMINDS US THAT OUR ABILITY TO GAIN WEALTH OR SUCCESS COMES FROM GOD. HE GIVES US THAT POWER TO BUILD SOMETHING THAT SERVES OTHERS AND FULFILLS HIS PROMISES. ENTREPRENEURSHIP IN THE KINGDOM ISN'T JUST A CAREER–IT'S A CALLING.

LIKE JOSEPH, YOU DON'T NEED TO START WITH A SPOTLIGHT. YOU NEED TO START WITH OBEDIENCE. WHETHER YOU'RE MANAGING A TEAM, RUNNING A SMALL BUSINESS, OR DREAMING OF ONE, LEAD WITH PURPOSE, GENEROSITY, AND TRUST IN GOD.

KEY POINTS

- GOD GIVES THE POWER TO BUILD AND CREATE.
- PURPOSE AND GENEROSITY MATTER MORE THAN PROFIT.
- KINGDOM LEADERSHIP REFLECTS GOD'S HEART IN EVERY DECISION.

DEAR GOD,
THANK YOU FOR BLESSING ME WITH VISION, GIFTS, AND OPPORTUNITY. HELP ME TO LEAD WITH INTEGRITY AND TO REFLECT YOUR LOVE IN EVERYTHING I DO. REMIND ME THAT MY BUSINESS IS YOURS, AND I'M HERE TO SERVE OTHERS THROUGH IT. GUIDE MY DECISIONS AND HELP ME TRUST YOU IN EVERY SEASON. MAY MY WORK BRING HOPE, SERVE PEOPLE WELL, AND HONOR YOU. IN JESUS' NAME, AMEN.

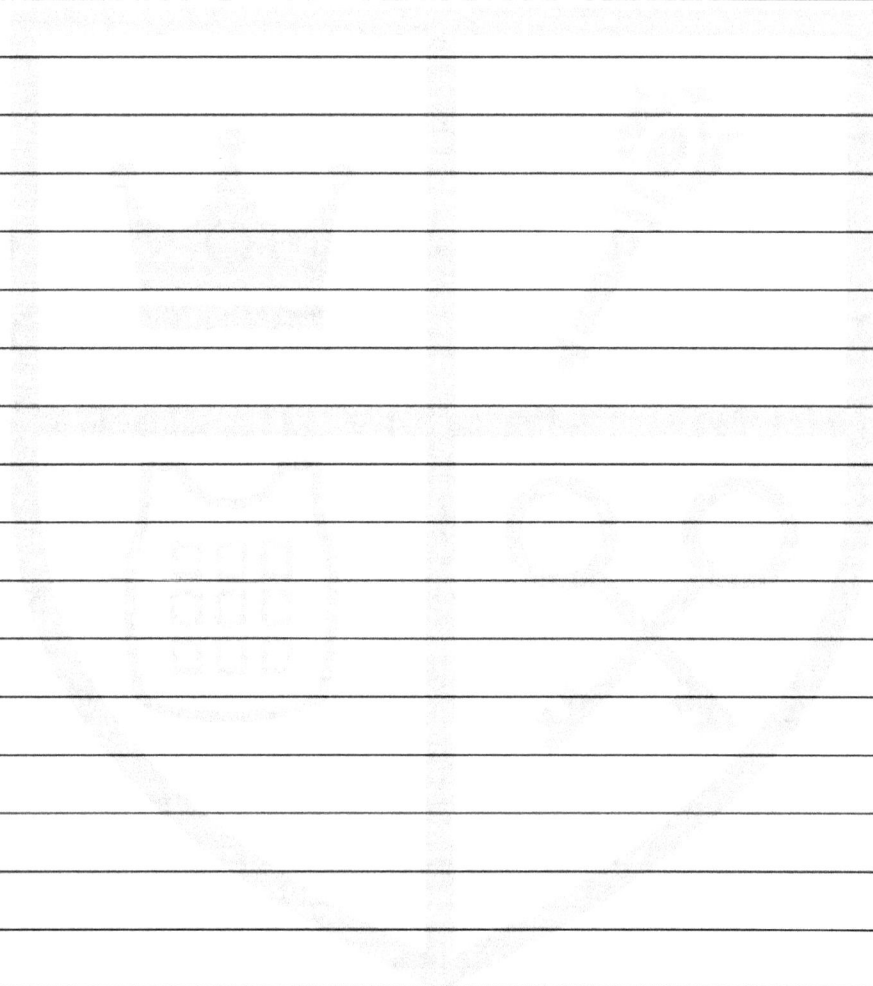

"WHATEVER YOU DO, DO IT HEARTILY, AS TO THE LORD AND NOT TO MEN."

–COLOSSIANS 3:23 (NKJV)

DEVOTIONAL READING

KINGDOM ENTREPRENEURSHIP DOESN'T JUST RELY ON CREATIVITY—IT THRIVES ON STRATEGY. JOSEPH DIDN'T JUST INTERPRET PHARAOH'S DREAMS—HE CREATED A PLAN. HE STORED FOOD DURING GOOD YEARS TO PREPARE FOR FAMINE. HIS FAITH WORKED HAND-IN-HAND WITH WISDOM.

GOD CALLS US TO USE BOTH PRAYER AND PLANNING. AS PROVERBS 16:9 SAYS, "A MAN'S HEART PLANS HIS WAY, BUT THE LORD DIRECTS HIS STEPS." THAT MEANS WE PREPARE WITH CARE, BUT TRUST GOD TO GUIDE THE OUTCOME. WHEN WE LEAD WITH DILIGENCE AND DEPENDENCE ON GOD, WE BUILD THINGS THAT LAST.

LIKE JOSEPH, WE CAN PREPARE, SERVE, AND LEAD IN A WAY THAT BRINGS LIFE TO OTHERS. WE'RE NOT BUILDING JUST FOR OURSELVES—WE'RE BUILDING TO BLESS FAMILIES, COMMUNITIES, AND GENERATIONS.

DAILY REFLECTION
Daily Reflection

Today,

ARE YOU CREATING A PLAN THAT ALIGNS WITH GOD'S PURPOSE FOR YOUR WORK?

_____
_____
_____
_____
_____
_____

Today,

HOW CAN STRATEGY AND PRAYER WORK TOGETHER IN YOUR BUSINESS OR LEADERSHIP?

_____
_____
_____
_____
_____
_____

Today,

WHAT'S ONE WISE STEP YOU CAN TAKE THIS WEEK TO STRENGTHEN YOUR GOD-GIVEN ASSIGNMENT?

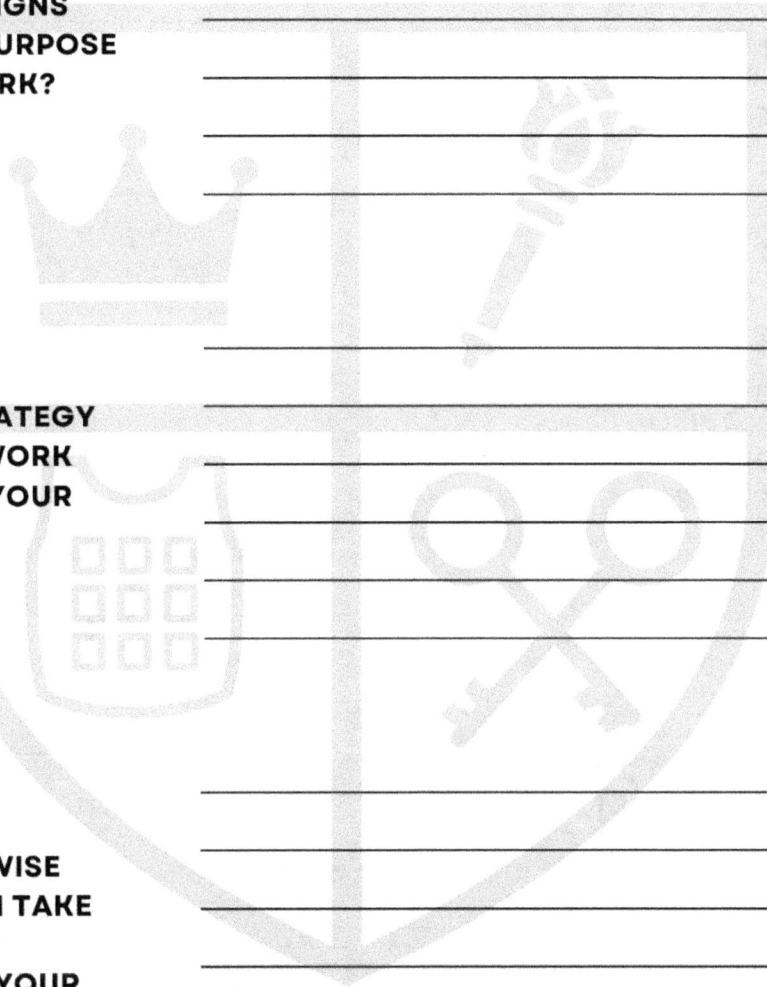

_____
_____
_____
_____
_____

**WRITE THE VISION:
TAKE TIME THIS WEEK
TO OUTLINE A PLAN
FOR YOUR GOD-GIVEN
IDEA. ASK FOR HIS
GUIDANCE.**

_____
_____
_____
_____
_____

**SEEK WISE COUNSEL:
TALK TO A MENTOR OR
TRUSTED ADVISOR
ABOUT YOUR VISION
AND GET FEEDBACK.**

_____
_____
_____
_____

**TAKE ONE BOLD STEP:
ACT ON ONE PART OF
YOUR PLAN THIS WEEK,
TRUSTING GOD TO
BLESS YOUR
OBEDIENCE.**

_____
_____
_____
_____
_____

LEAD WITH COMPASSION, NOT CONTROL.

SCRIPTURE MEDITATION

"COMMIT YOUR WORKS TO THE LORD, AND YOUR THOUGHTS WILL BE ESTABLISHED."
—PROVERBS 16:3 (NKJV)

MEDITATION REFLECTION

GOD CARES ABOUT EVERY PART OF YOUR WORK. HE'S NOT JUST WITH YOU IN CHURCH—HE'S WITH YOU IN MEETINGS, PROJECTS, AND PLANNING SESSIONS. WHEN YOU COMMIT YOUR PLANS TO HIM, HE PROMISES TO GUIDE YOU.

JOSEPH'S INFLUENCE DIDN'T COME FROM GUESSING. IT CAME FROM LISTENING TO GOD AND ACTING WITH WISDOM. WE CAN DO THE SAME. EVERY KINGDOM VISION NEEDS STRUCTURE, PRAYER, AND CONSISTENCY TO GROW.

DON'T RUSH THE PROCESS. ASK GOD FOR STRATEGY. LISTEN FOR HIS VOICE IN BOTH THE BIG DREAMS AND THE DAILY STEPS. WHEN YOUR HEART STAYS FOCUSED ON HIM, HE WILL DIRECT YOUR EVERY MOVE.

KEY POINTS

- GOD BLESSES STRATEGY ROOTED IN PRAYER.
- PLANNING AND FAITH GO HAND IN HAND.
- LEADING WELL STARTS WITH LISTENING TO GOD.

DEAR GOD,
THANK YOU FOR THE VISION YOU'VE PLACED IN MY HEART. HELP ME PLAN WISELY, LISTEN CLOSELY, AND MOVE BOLDLY IN FAITH. I COMMIT MY IDEAS AND EFFORTS TO YOU. LEAD ME IN WISDOM AND GIVE ME DIVINE STRATEGY TO BUILD WHAT YOU'VE CALLED ME TO. MAY MY PLANS REFLECT YOUR HEART, AND MAY EVERY STEP BE LED BY YOUR SPIRIT.
IN JESUS' NAME, AMEN.

JOURNAL REFLECTION-NEXT STEPS
Journal Reflection-Next Steps

"THEN PHARAOH SAID TO JOSEPH, 'INASMUCH AS GOD HAS SHOWN YOU ALL THIS, THERE IS NO ONE AS DISCERNING AND WISE AS YOU. YOU SHALL BE OVER MY HOUSE, AND ALL MY PEOPLE SHALL BE RULED ACCORDING TO YOUR WORD; ONLY IN REGARD TO THE THRONE WILL I BE GREATER THAN YOU.'"

–GENESIS 41:39–40 (NKJV)

DEVOTIONAL READING

JOSEPH DIDN'T CHASE AFTER TITLES OR RECOGNITION. HE SIMPLY STAYED FAITHFUL IN EVERY PLACE GOD PUT HIM. FROM THE PIT TO THE PALACE, JOSEPH WALKED IN WISDOM, OBEDIENCE, AND HUMILITY. HIS STORY REMINDS US THAT GOD RAISES UP LEADERS IN HIS PERFECT TIME.

JOSEPH CARRIED WHAT WE NOW CALL A LEADERSHIP MANTLE—A SPIRITUAL ASSIGNMENT TO LEAD, INFLUENCE, AND SERVE. THIS FOURFOLD MANTLE INCLUDED KINGSHIP, RULERSHIP, PRIESTHOOD, AND AMBASSADORSHIP. HE DIDN'T USE POWER FOR SELFISH GAIN. HE GOVERNED WISELY, LIVED PURELY, AND POINTED OTHERS TO GOD. THAT'S THE KIND OF LEADER GOD IS STILL LOOKING FOR TODAY.

JOSEPH'S LIFE CHALLENGES US TO LEAD LIKE HE DID—WITH VISION, INTEGRITY, AND PURPOSE. YOU DON'T NEED A TITLE TO CARRY THIS MANTLE. IF YOU'RE SERVING OTHERS, INFLUENCING LIVES, OR STANDING FOR TRUTH, YOU'RE ALREADY WALKING IN LEADERSHIP. TRUST GOD TO GUIDE YOU, AND STAY FAITHFUL WHERE YOU ARE.

Today,

**WHAT LEADERSHIP
QUALITY FROM
JOSEPH'S LIFE CAN YOU
APPLY TO YOUR OWN
LIFE TODAY?**

_____
_____
_____
_____
_____
_____

Today,

**DO YOU SEE YOUR
CURRENT ROLE AS A
TRAINING GROUND FOR
GREATER LEADERSHIP?**

_____
_____
_____
_____
_____
_____

Today,

**HOW CAN YOU LEAD
WITH BOTH HUMILITY
AND BOLDNESS THIS
WEEK?**

_____
_____
_____
_____
_____
_____

PICK A TRAIT TO PRACTICE: CHOOSE ONE ASPECT OF JOSEPH'S LEADERSHIP—LIKE INTEGRITY, DISCERNMENT, OR WISDOM—AND FOCUS ON IT THIS WEEK.

_____
_____
_____
_____
_____
_____

SERVE WHERE YOU ARE: FIND ONE WAY TO LEAD WITH LOVE AND PURPOSE IN YOUR CURRENT SETTING.

_____
_____
_____
_____
_____

PRAY FOR THE MANTLE: ASK GOD TO GROW YOU IN LEADERSHIP AND HELP YOU CARRY THE JOSEPH MANTLE WITH FAITHFULNESS.

_____
_____
_____
_____
_____

GRACE IS YOUR STRENGTH WHEN YOU FEEL WEAK.

SCRIPTURE MEDITATION

"TO HIM WHO LOVED US AND WASHED US FROM OUR SINS IN HIS OWN BLOOD, AND HAS MADE US KINGS AND PRIESTS TO HIS GOD AND FATHER..."
—REVELATION 1:5-6 (NKJV)

MEDITATION REFLECTION

JOSEPH DIDN'T JUST RECEIVE AN EARTHLY PROMOTION—HE STEPPED INTO A DIVINE CALLING. THE SAME IS TRUE FOR YOU. REVELATION SAYS THAT GOD HAS MADE US KINGS AND PRIESTS. THAT MEANS WE'RE CALLED TO LEAD WITH WISDOM AND LIVE CLOSE TO GOD.

THE JOSEPH MANTLE IS ABOUT USING YOUR INFLUENCE TO SERVE AND YOUR CHARACTER TO POINT PEOPLE BACK TO GOD. JOSEPH STAYED STRONG IN EVERY SEASON—NOT BECAUSE HE HAD EVERYTHING FIGURED OUT, BUT BECAUSE HE WALKED WITH GOD. HE BROUGHT HEAVEN'S WISDOM INTO EGYPT'S SYSTEMS. YOU CAN BRING KINGDOM INFLUENCE WHEREVER GOD PLACES YOU TOO.

LET THIS TRUTH ENCOURAGE YOU: YOU ARE CHOSEN, EQUIPPED, AND SENT. YOUR DAILY OBEDIENCE IS SHAPING YOUR LEGACY. THE MANTLE IS NOT ABOUT BEING PERFECT—IT'S ABOUT BEING FAITHFUL.

KEY POINTS

- THE JOSEPH MANTLE IS A SPIRITUAL LEADERSHIP CALLING.
- GOD CALLS US TO LEAD WITH WISDOM, INTEGRITY, AND LOVE.
- DAILY FAITHFULNESS SHAPES LONG-TERM INFLUENCE.

DAILY PRAYER
Daily Prayer

DEAR GOD,
THANK YOU FOR THE EXAMPLE OF
JOSEPH. HELP ME TO LEAD WITH
WISDOM, WALK IN HUMILITY, AND
STAY FAITHFUL IN EVERY SEASON. I
RECEIVE THE MANTLE YOU'VE
PLACED ON MY LIFE—TO LEAD, SERVE,
AND INFLUENCE FOR YOUR GLORY.
GROW ME INTO A LEADER WHO
REFLECTS YOUR HEART. TEACH ME
HOW TO CARRY THIS ASSIGNMENT
WITH GRACE, STRENGTH, AND
COURAGE. MAY MY LEADERSHIP BE
MARKED BY YOUR SPIRIT AND
CENTERED IN YOUR TRUTH.
IN JESUS' NAME, AMEN.

JOURNAL REFLECTION-NEXT STEPS
Journal Reflection-Next Steps

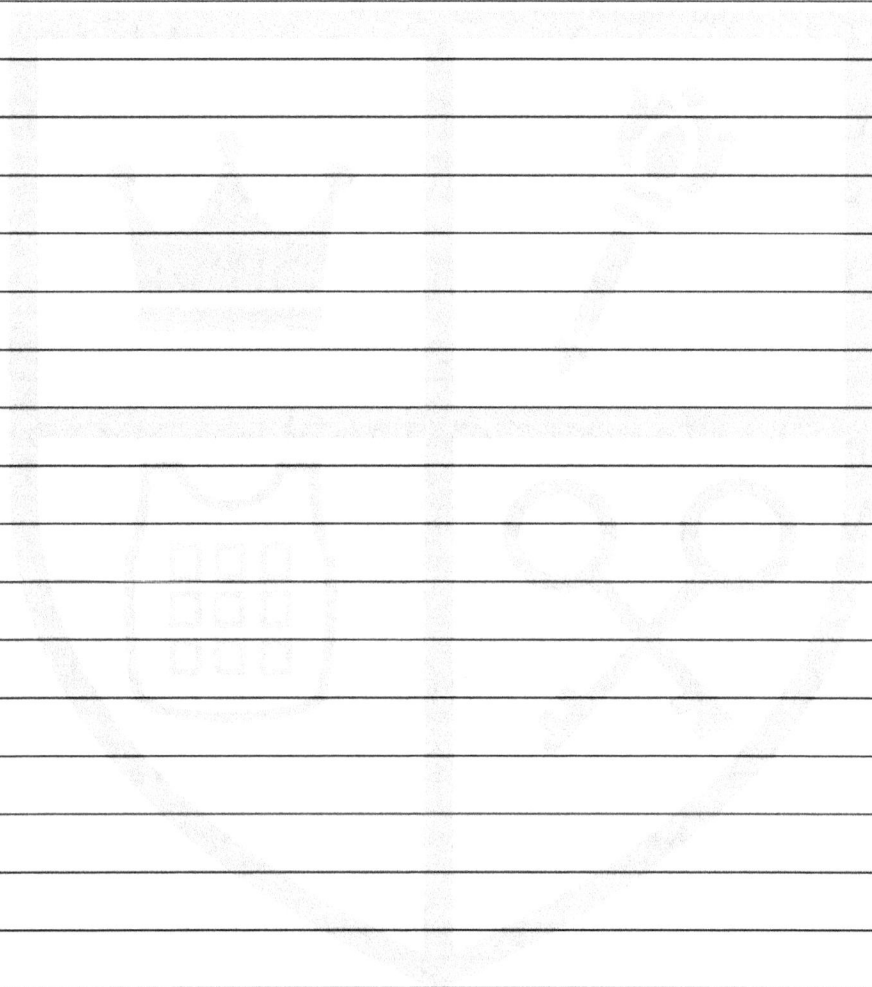

"YOU SHALL BE OVER MY HOUSE, AND ALL MY PEOPLE SHALL BE RULED ACCORDING TO YOUR WORD; ONLY IN REGARD TO THE THRONE WILL I BE GREATER THAN YOU."
–GENESIS 41:40 (NKJV)

DEVOTIONAL READING

JOSEPH DIDN'T GET TO THE PALACE BY LUCK. HE WAS PREPARED THROUGH YEARS OF SERVICE, STRUGGLE, AND TRUST. WHEN THE OPPORTUNITY CAME, HE DIDN'T PANIC OR SHRINK BACK. HE WALKED IN GOD-GIVEN WISDOM AND INFLUENCE. PHARAOH SAW SOMETHING DIFFERENT IN JOSEPH—HE SAW THE SPIRIT OF GOD AT WORK.

TODAY, GOD IS STILL LOOKING FOR LEADERS LIKE THAT. YOU DON'T HAVE TO BE PERFECT. YOU JUST HAVE TO BE AVAILABLE, OBEDIENT, AND FAITHFUL. WHEN YOU STAY CLOSE TO GOD AND GROW YOUR GIFTS, HE WILL BRING INFLUENCE IN HIS PERFECT TIMING. REMEMBER, LEADERSHIP ISN'T ABOUT BEING IN CHARGE—IT'S ABOUT SERVING OTHERS WITH WISDOM AND GRACE.

JOSEPH TEACHES US TO WALK IN WISDOM, MANAGE WELL, FORGIVE FREELY, AND LEAD WITH VISION. WHETHER YOU LEAD IN YOUR HOME, YOUR JOB, OR YOUR MINISTRY, LET YOUR INFLUENCE BE SHAPED BY GOD'S HEART. HE IS THE ONE WHO OPENS DOORS AND EQUIPS YOU FOR THE JOURNEY AHEAD.

DAILY REFLECTION
Daily Reflection

Today,

WHAT AREA OF YOUR LIFE REQUIRES MORE OF GOD'S WISDOM RIGHT NOW?

_____
_____
_____
_____
_____
_____

Today,

HOW CAN YOU USE YOUR INFLUENCE TO SERVE AND UPLIFT OTHERS THIS WEEK?

_____
_____
_____
_____
_____
_____

Today,

ARE YOU PREPARING YOUR HEART AND HABITS FOR GREATER RESPONSIBILITY?

_____
_____
_____
_____
_____
_____

PRAY FOR WISDOM: ASK GOD FOR UNDERSTANDING AND DISCERNMENT IN YOUR LEADERSHIP DECISIONS.

_____
_____
_____
_____
_____
_____

LEAD WITH LOVE: LOOK FOR ONE OPPORTUNITY TO LEAD SOMEONE WITH ENCOURAGEMENT, PATIENCE, OR GRACE.

_____
_____
_____
_____
_____

TRUST GOD'S TIMING: WRITE DOWN ONE THING YOU'RE WAITING ON AND SURRENDER IT TO GOD IN PRAYER.

_____
_____
_____
_____
_____

GOD'S TIMING IS ALWAYS ON TIME.

SCRIPTURE MEDITATION

"IF ANY OF YOU LACKS WISDOM, LET HIM ASK OF GOD, WHO GIVES TO ALL LIBERALLY AND WITHOUT REPROACH, AND IT WILL BE GIVEN TO HIM."
—JAMES 1:5 (NKJV)

MEDITATION REFLECTION

WISDOM IS ONE OF THE GREATEST TOOLS IN A LEADER'S LIFE. JOSEPH DIDN'T JUST LEAD WITH AUTHORITY—HE LED WITH WISDOM. THAT WISDOM DIDN'T COME FROM BOOKS OR PEOPLE ALONE—IT CAME FROM GOD. WHEN WE ASK GOD FOR WISDOM, HE PROMISES TO GIVE IT GENEROUSLY.

YOU MAY BE FACING NEW CHALLENGES OR WAITING FOR CLARITY. ASK GOD FOR WISDOM, AND HE WILL GUIDE YOUR STEPS. LEADERSHIP ROOTED IN PRAYER IS STEADY, STRONG, AND SPIRIT-LED. DON'T RELY ONLY ON YOUR STRENGTH—RELY ON HIS GUIDANCE.

JUST AS JOSEPH LED A NATION WITH GOD'S HELP, YOU CAN LEAD IN YOUR SPHERE OF INFLUENCE WITH GOD'S WISDOM. STAY CONNECTED TO HIM, AND HE WILL SHOW YOU THE WAY.

KEY POINTS

- WISDOM COMES FROM GOD AND IS AVAILABLE TO EVERY BELIEVER.
- LEADERSHIP IS ABOUT STEWARDSHIP, SERVICE, AND INFLUENCE.
- GOD EQUIPS THOSE WHO WALK WITH HIM IN HUMILITY.

DEAR GOD,
I ASK YOU TODAY FOR WISDOM. HELP ME LEAD WITH GRACE, PATIENCE, AND CLARITY. LET MY DECISIONS REFLECT YOUR WILL, AND LET MY ACTIONS POINT OTHERS TO YOU. USE ME TO MAKE A DIFFERENCE RIGHT WHERE I AM. I SURRENDER EVERY RESPONSIBILITY, DREAM, AND OPPORTUNITY TO YOU. TEACH ME HOW TO STEWARD WHAT YOU'VE PLACED IN MY HANDS. LET MY INFLUENCE REFLECT YOUR TRUTH AND LOVE.
THANK YOU FOR EQUIPPING ME FOR SUCH A TIME AS THIS. I TRUST YOU TO GUIDE ME EVERY STEP OF THE WAY.
IN JESUS' NAME, AMEN.

JOURNAL REFLECTION-NEXT STEPS
Journal Reflection-Next Steps

"BUT THE WISDOM THAT IS FROM ABOVE IS FIRST PURE, THEN PEACEABLE, GENTLE, WILLING TO YIELD, FULL OF MERCY AND GOOD FRUITS, WITHOUT PARTIALITY AND WITHOUT HYPOCRISY."

–JAMES 3:17 (NKJV)

DEVOTIONAL READING

JOSEPH'S PROMOTION CAME WITH POWER, BUT HE DIDN'T LEAD FOR HIMSELF—HE LED FOR OTHERS. PHARAOH GAVE HIM FULL AUTHORITY OVER EGYPT, YET JOSEPH USED THAT ROLE TO SERVE DURING THE FAMINE. HE CREATED A PLAN THAT SAVED COUNTLESS LIVES. HIS LEADERSHIP WAS ROOTED IN SERVICE, NOT STATUS.

JOSEPH CREDITED GOD FOR HIS WISDOM. WHEN PHARAOH NEEDED ANSWERS, JOSEPH SAID, "IT IS NOT IN ME; GOD WILL GIVE PHARAOH AN ANSWER OF PEACE" (GENESIS 41:16). THIS KIND OF WISDOM DOESN'T COME FROM THE WORLD—IT COMES FROM WALKING CLOSELY WITH GOD. ECCLESIASTES 10:10 REMINDS US THAT WISDOM MAKES OUR WORK EFFECTIVE: "WISDOM BRINGS SUCCESS."

EVEN AFTER JOSEPH GAINED INFLUENCE, HE STAYED HUMBLE. HE FORGAVE THOSE WHO HURT HIM AND GAVE GOD THE GLORY FOR EVERY VICTORY. TRUE SUCCESS DOESN'T LEAD TO PRIDE. IT LEADS TO DEEPER FAITH, GREATER COMPASSION, AND A DESIRE TO USE INFLUENCE TO BLESS OTHERS.

Today,

ARE THERE AREAS IN YOUR LEADERSHIP WHERE PRIDE OR CONTROL HAS TAKEN THE LEAD?

_____
_____
_____
_____
_____
_____
_____

Today,

IHOW CAN YOU SHOW HUMILITY, INTEGRITY, AND COMPASSION AS YOUR INFLUENCE GROWS?

_____
_____
_____
_____
_____
_____

Today,

WHAT'S ONE RECENT DECISION WHERE YOU NEED TO INVITE GOD'S WISDOM TO MAKE SURE IT REFLECTS HIS WILL?

_____
_____
_____
_____
_____

LET GO OF PRIDE: IDENTIFY ONE AREA WHERE YOU'RE TEMPTED TO LEAD IN YOUR OWN STRENGTH. SURRENDER IT TO GOD.

_____
_____
_____
_____
_____

SEEK ACCOUNTABILITY: ASK A TRUSTED FRIEND OR MENTOR TO HELP YOU STAY GROUNDED IN GODLY VALUES.

_____
_____
_____
_____

MODEL JOSEPH'S HUMILITY: THIS WEEK, CHOOSE ONE ACTION THAT REFLECTS JOSEPH'S HEART TO SERVE AND HONOR GOD.

_____
_____
_____
_____
_____

WHERE THERE IS VISION, THERE IS PROVISION.

SCRIPTURE MEDITATION

"HE HAS SHOWN YOU, O MAN, WHAT IS GOOD; AND WHAT DOES THE LORD REQUIRE OF YOU BUT TO DO JUSTLY, TO LOVE MERCY, AND TO WALK HUMBLY WITH YOUR GOD?"
—MICAH 6:8 (NKJV)

MEDITATION REFLECTION

JOSEPH'S LEADERSHIP WAS MARKED BY HUMILITY AND WISDOM. THOUGH HE HAD POWER, HE USED IT TO SERVE OTHERS, SAVE LIVES, AND GIVE GLORY TO GOD. HE SHOWS US THAT GODLY LEADERSHIP IS ROOTED IN CHARACTER.

MICAH 6:8 REMINDS US WHAT GOD VALUES MOST IN LEADERS: JUSTICE, MERCY, AND HUMILITY. THESE TRAITS DON'T ALWAYS GET APPLAUSE, BUT THEY BUILD TRUST AND REFLECT GOD'S HEART. WHEN WE LEAD WITH HUMILITY, WE INVITE GOD INTO EVERY PART OF OUR JOURNEY.

LET SUCCESS REFINE YOUR HEART—NOT INFLATE YOUR EGO. THE MORE INFLUENCE YOU GAIN, THE MORE YOU NEED GOD'S WISDOM TO LEAD WELL. HUMILITY IS THE FOUNDATION OF LASTING LEADERSHIP.

KEY POINTS
- HUMILITY GUARDS YOUR HEART AS INFLUENCE GROWS.
- LEADERSHIP IS A STEWARDSHIP, NOT OWNERSHIP.
- WISDOM FROM GOD LEADS TO FAIR AND FRUITFUL LEADERSHIP.

DEAR GOD,
THANK YOU FOR JOSEPH'S EXAMPLE OF HUMBLE, FAITHFUL LEADERSHIP. HELP ME LEAD LIKE HE DID—WITH COMPASSION, WISDOM, AND A HEART THAT POINTS OTHERS TO YOU. KEEP ME FROM PRIDE, AND REMIND ME DAILY THAT ALL I HAVE COMES FROM YOU. GIVE ME YOUR WISDOM IN EVERY DECISION, AND USE MY INFLUENCE TO BLESS OTHERS. HELP ME LEAD NOT JUST WITH SKILL, BUT WITH CHARACTER.
IN JESUS' NAME, AMEN.

JOURNAL REFLECTION-NEXT STEPS
Journal Reflection-Next Steps

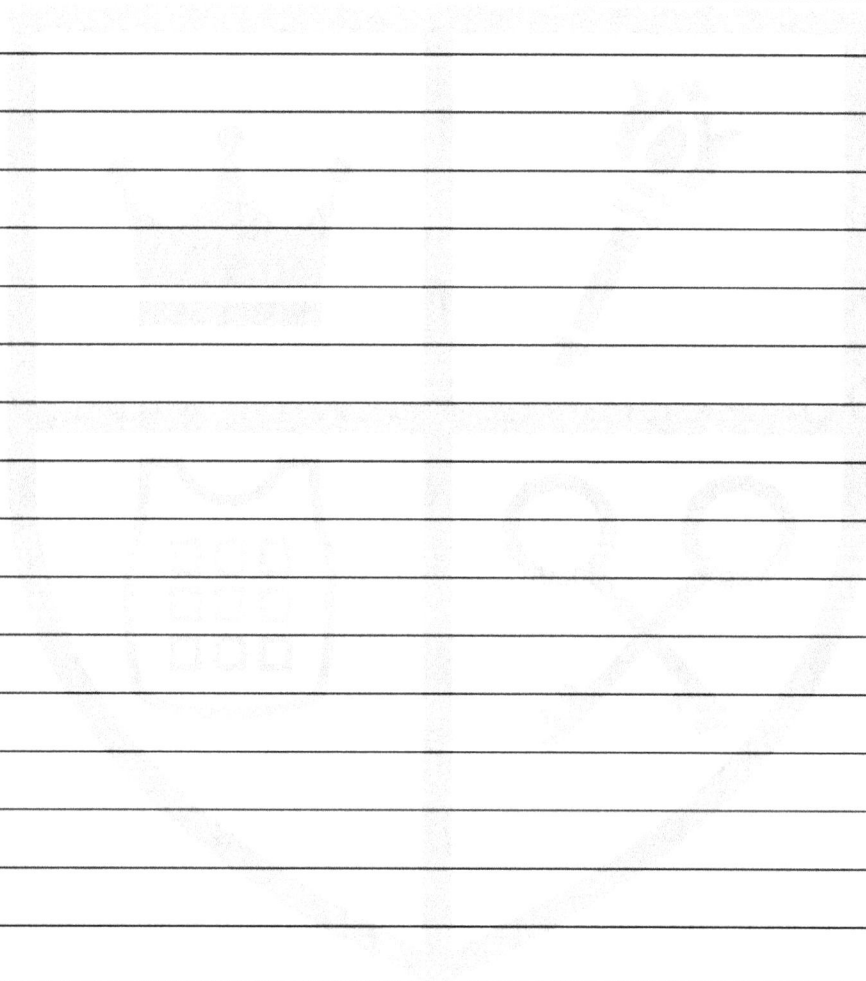

"THEN PHARAOH SAID TO JOSEPH, 'SEE, I HAVE SET YOU OVER ALL THE LAND OF EGYPT.'"

–GENESIS 41:41 (NKJV)

DEVOTIONAL READING

JOSEPH DIDN'T CHASE PROMOTION—HE PREPARED FOR IT. HE WAS FAITHFUL IN EVERY SEASON: AS A SLAVE, A PRISONER, AND NOW AS EGYPT'S SECOND-IN-COMMAND. PHARAOH HONORED JOSEPH'S WISDOM AND GAVE HIM LEADERSHIP BECAUSE HE COULD BE TRUSTED.

LEADERSHIP IS NOT JUST ABOUT REACHING THE TOP. IT'S ABOUT HOW YOU LEAD ONCE YOU GET THERE. JOSEPH DIDN'T USE HIS TITLE FOR REVENGE OR PERSONAL COMFORT. HE USED IT TO BLESS NATIONS. THAT'S WHAT KINGDOM LEADERSHIP LOOKS LIKE.

TRUE LEADERS DON'T FORGET WHERE THEY CAME FROM. THEY REMEMBER WHO CALLED THEM AND WHY THEY SERVE. JOSEPH'S HEART STAYED SOFT, AND HIS VISION STAYED FOCUSED ON GOD'S PURPOSE. THAT'S WHY HIS LEADERSHIP LASTED.

DAILY REFLECTION
Daily Reflection

Today,

HOW DO YOU VIEW YOUR CURRENT ROLE— AS A PLATFORM OR A PLACE OF PURPOSE?

_____
_____
_____
_____
_____
_____

Today,

WHAT DOES IT MEAN TO YOU TO STEWARD SUCCESS FOR GOD'S GLORY?

_____
_____
_____
_____
_____
_____

Today,

HOW CAN YOU BLESS OTHERS THROUGH YOUR LEADERSHIP THIS WEEK?

_____
_____
_____
_____
_____

SERVE INTENTIONALLY: LOOK FOR WAYS TO USE YOUR ROLE TO LIFT OTHERS UP OR SOLVE A PROBLEM.

_____
_____
_____
_____
_____
_____

REMEMBER YOUR SOURCE: REFLECT ON HOW GOD BROUGHT YOU TO WHERE YOU ARE.

_____
_____
_____
_____
_____

LEAD WITH A KINGDOM HEART: ASK GOD TO KEEP YOUR HEART SOFT AND YOUR VISION ALIGNED WITH HIS PURPOSE.

_____
_____
_____
_____
_____

TRUST GOD'S YES, AND TRUST HIS NO.

SCRIPTURE MEDITATION

"WHATEVER YOU DO, DO IT HEARTILY, AS TO THE LORD AND NOT TO MEN."
–COLOSSIANS 3:23 (NKJV)

MEDITATION REFLECTION

WHEN GOD GIVES US INFLUENCE, IT'S NEVER JUST FOR US. JOSEPH REMEMBERED THAT. HE HONORED PHARAOH, HELPED PEOPLE, AND STAYED FAITHFUL TO GOD. HIS LEADERSHIP MADE A DIFFERENCE BECAUSE IT CAME FROM A PURE HEART.

COLOSSIANS 3:23 REMINDS US THAT EVERYTHING WE DO IS FOR THE LORD. THIS INCLUDES BUSINESS, SCHOOL, MINISTRY, AND LEADERSHIP. WHEN WE DO OUR WORK AS AN OFFERING TO GOD, IT CHANGES HOW WE LEAD AND HOW WE LIVE.

DON'T BE DISCOURAGED BY SMALL BEGINNINGS OR OVERWHELMED BY BIG OPPORTUNITIES. STAY FAITHFUL, SERVE WITH JOY, AND TRUST THAT GOD IS USING EVERY MOMENT TO WRITE A BIGGER STORY THROUGH YOU.

KEY POINTS
- SUCCESS IS NOT THE GOAL—FAITHFULNESS IS.
- INFLUENCE IS AN OPPORTUNITY TO SERVE.
- EVERY ROLE IS SACRED WHEN DONE FOR GOD'S GLORY.

DEAR GOD,
THANK YOU FOR EVERY OPPORTUNITY TO LEAD AND SERVE. HELP ME TO SEE SUCCESS NOT AS A TROPHY, BUT AS A TOOL TO HELP OTHERS. KEEP MY HEART SOFT AND MY MIND FOCUSED ON YOUR KINGDOM. LET EVERY DECISION I MAKE HONOR YOU AND POINT PEOPLE TO YOUR GOODNESS. TEACH ME TO LEAD WITH WISDOM, LOVE, AND HUMILITY. IN JESUS' NAME, AMEN.

JOURNAL REFLECTION-NEXT STEPS
Journal Reflection-Next Steps

"AND BE KIND TO ONE ANOTHER, TENDERHEARTED, FORGIVING ONE ANOTHER, EVEN AS GOD IN CHRIST FORGAVE YOU."

–EPHESIANS 4:32 (NKJV)

DEVOTIONAL READING

LEADERSHIP BEGINS WITH PEOPLE, NOT JUST PROGRESS. JOSEPH'S STORY SHOWS US THE HEART OF LEADERSHIP ROOTED IN FORGIVENESS. HIS BROTHERS BETRAYED HIM, SOLD HIM, AND FORGOT HIM. YET, WHEN JOSEPH SAW THEM YEARS LATER, HE DIDN'T SEEK REVENGE—HE FORGAVE. "BUT NOW, DO NOT BE GRIEVED... FOR GOD SENT ME BEFORE YOU TO PRESERVE LIFE" (GENESIS 45:5). JOSEPH LED WITH A HEALED HEART, NOT A HARDENED ONE.

FORGIVENESS IS A LEADERSHIP TOOL. WITHOUT IT, BITTERNESS GROWS AND CLOUDS OUR ABILITY TO GUIDE OTHERS WELL. BUT FORGIVENESS FREES US TO LEAD WITH LOVE. JOSEPH PROVIDED FOOD AND SHELTER FOR HIS BROTHERS—THE VERY ONES WHO HURT HIM. HE SHOWED GRACE IN ACTION, CHOOSING TO RESTORE RATHER THAN RETALIATE.

HEALING AND LEADERSHIP GO HAND IN HAND. JOSEPH HAD ALREADY DONE THE INNER WORK BEFORE HE FACED HIS BROTHERS AGAIN. THAT'S WHY HE COULD LEAD WITH STRENGTH AND COMPASSION. GREAT LEADERS FORGIVE EVEN WHEN IT'S HARD, BECAUSE HEALING BRINGS PEACE—FOR YOU AND THOSE YOU LEAD.

Today,

**IS THERE SOMEONE
YOU NEED TO FORGIVE
SO YOU CAN LEAD
WITH FREEDOM?**

_____
_____
_____
_____
_____
_____

Today,

**WHAT RELATIONSHIPS
IN YOUR LIFE NEED
HEALING?**

_____
_____
_____
_____
_____
_____

Today,

**HOW HAS
FORGIVENESS SHAPED
YOUR GROWTH AS A
LEADER?**

_____
_____
_____
_____
_____
_____

FAITH IN MOTION
Faith in Motion

ASK FOR HEALING: INVITE GOD TO HEAL ANY HURT OR BETRAYAL THAT STILL WEIGHS ON YOUR HEART.

_____
_____
_____
_____
_____
_____

CHOOSE FORGIVENESS: DECIDE TO FORGIVE SOMEONE TODAY—NOT BECAUSE THEY DESERVE IT, BUT BECAUSE GOD HAS FORGIVEN YOU.

_____
_____
_____
_____
_____

LEAD WITH COMPASSION: PRACTICE KINDNESS TOWARD SOMEONE YOU'VE STRUGGLED WITH. LET HEALING SHAPE YOUR LEADERSHIP.

_____
_____
_____
_____
_____

DON'T COMPARE YOUR JOURNEY—GOD'S PATH FOR YOU IS UNIQUE.

SCRIPTURE MEDITATION

"BELOVED, I PRAY THAT YOU MAY PROSPER IN ALL THINGS AND BE IN HEALTH, JUST AS YOUR SOUL PROSPERS."
—3 JOHN 2 (NKJV)

MEDITATION REFLECTION

HEALING AND FORGIVENESS GO HAND IN HAND. JOSEPH'S SOUL PROSPERED EVEN IN HARDSHIP BECAUSE HE LET GOD DO THE HEALING. HE DIDN'T WAIT FOR AN APOLOGY—HE LED WITH MERCY. THAT DECISION BROUGHT UNITY TO A BROKEN FAMILY.

FORGIVENESS IS A GIFT YOU GIVE TO YOURSELF AND OTHERS. IT OPENS THE DOOR TO GRACE, REBUILDS TRUST, AND CREATES ROOM FOR REAL CONNECTION. LEADERSHIP THAT FLOWS FROM A HEALED HEART BRINGS LASTING PEACE.

KEY POINTS

- FORGIVENESS HEALS YOU FIRST, THEN OTHERS.
- A HEALED LEADER BUILDS STRONGER RELATIONSHIPS.
- GRACE IS A FOUNDATION FOR HEALTHY LEADERSHIP.

DEAR GOD,
THANK YOU FOR SHOWING ME THROUGH JOSEPH THAT FORGIVENESS LEADS TO PEACE. HEAL THE PLACES IN MY HEART WHERE PAIN STILL LIVES. HELP ME TO FORGIVE FREELY AND LEAD WITH LOVE. LET MY LEADERSHIP BRING UNITY, NOT DIVISION. USE ME TO RESTORE WHAT'S BEEN BROKEN, AND HELP ME WALK IN THE FREEDOM YOU OFFER.
IN JESUS' NAME, AMEN.

JOURNAL REFLECTION-NEXT STEPS
Journal Reflection-Next Steps

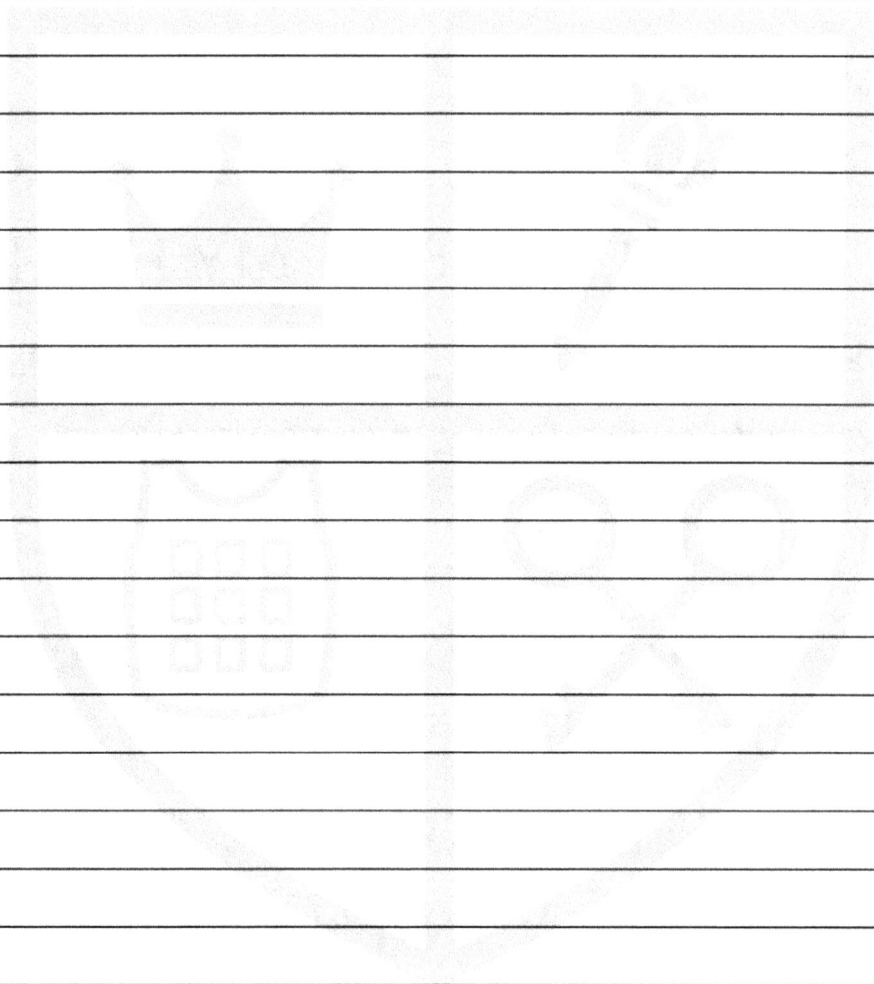

"LET ALL BITTERNESS, WRATH, ANGER, CLAMOR, AND EVIL SPEAKING BE PUT AWAY FROM YOU... FORGIVING ONE ANOTHER, EVEN AS GOD IN CHRIST FORGAVE YOU."

—EPHESIANS 4:31–32 (NKJV)

DEVOTIONAL READING

FORGIVENESS DOESN'T STAY PRIVATE—IT BUILDS CULTURE. JOSEPH'S DECISION TO FORGIVE SHAPED HOW HIS FAMILY LIVED AND WORKED TOGETHER. HE DIDN'T EXCUSE THE BETRAYAL, BUT HE CHOSE RESTORATION. HE TOLD HIS BROTHERS, "YOU MEANT EVIL AGAINST ME, BUT GOD MEANT IT FOR GOOD" (GENESIS 50:20).

LEADERSHIP ROOTED IN GRACE ALLOWS OTHERS TO GROW. JOSEPH'S KINDNESS CREATED SAFETY, HEALED OLD WOUNDS, AND UNIFIED HIS FAMILY. WHEN LEADERS CHOOSE FORGIVENESS, THEY BUILD TRUST, MODEL HUMILITY, AND MAKE ROOM FOR SECOND CHANCES.

A FORGIVING LEADER REFLECTS THE HEART OF GOD. "EVEN AS CHRIST FORGAVE YOU…" (COLOSSIANS 3:13). WHEN WE LET GO OF GRUDGES AND WALK IN GRACE, WE INSPIRE THOSE AROUND US TO DO THE SAME. FORGIVENESS ISN'T WEAKNESS—IT'S STRENGTH THAT CHANGES EVERYTHING.

DAILY REFLECTION
Daily Reflection

Today,

ARE YOU MODELING FORGIVENESS IN YOUR LEADERSHIP?

_____
_____
_____
_____
_____
_____

Today,

HOW COULD GRACE CHANGE THE ATMOSPHERE IN YOUR HOME OR TEAM?

_____
_____
_____
_____
_____
_____

Today,

IWHAT DOES IT LOOK LIKE TO LEAD WITH MERCY AND TRUTH?

_____
_____
_____
_____
_____
_____

START WITH A CONVERSATION: REACH OUT TO SOMEONE YOU'VE BEEN DISTANT FROM. START FRESH WITH GRACE.

_____
_____
_____
_____
_____

CREATE A SAFE SPACE: BE A LEADER WHO ALLOWS MISTAKES AND OFFERS ROOM TO GROW.

_____
_____
_____
_____
_____

CREATE A SAFE SPACE: BE A LEADER WHO ALLOWS MISTAKES AND OFFERS ROOM TO GROW.

_____
_____
_____
_____
_____

INFLUENCE BEGINS WITH STEWARDSHIP, NOT SPOTLIGHT.

SCRIPTURE MEDITATION

"IF IT IS POSSIBLE, AS MUCH AS DEPENDS ON YOU, LIVE PEACEABLY WITH ALL MEN."
—ROMANS 12:18 (NKJV)

MEDITATION REFLECTION

YOU MAY NOT BE ABLE TO FIX EVERY RELATIONSHIP, BUT YOU CAN DO YOUR PART. LIVING IN PEACE IS POSSIBLE WHEN YOU LEAD WITH GRACE. JOSEPH MODELED PEACE—NOT BY IGNORING THE PAST, BUT BY CHOOSING TO FORGIVE AND LOVE IN THE PRESENT.

FORGIVENESS SETS THE TONE FOR HEALTHY LEADERSHIP. IT CHANGES YOUR ENVIRONMENT AND DRAWS PEOPLE CLOSER. WHEN YOU RELEASE OFFENSE, YOU CREATE SPACE FOR HEALING AND TRUST TO GROW. THAT'S THE POWER OF GODLY LEADERSHIP.

KEY POINTS

- FORGIVENESS SHAPES CULTURE AND COMMUNITY.
- CHOOSING PEACE IS PART OF KINGDOM LEADERSHIP.
- A GRACIOUS LEADER BUILDS LASTING TRUST.

DEAR GOD,
THANK YOU FOR THE POWER OF FORGIVENESS. HELP ME LEAD IN A WAY THAT BUILDS TRUST AND REFLECTS YOUR GRACE. LET MY LEADERSHIP BRING PEACE, NOT DIVISION. HELP ME CREATE AN ATMOSPHERE WHERE PEOPLE FEEL SAFE, VALUED, AND LOVED. USE MY WORDS AND ACTIONS TO BRING HEALING, AND LET MY LEADERSHIP MIRROR YOUR HEART.
IN JESUS' NAME, AMEN.

JOURNAL REFLECTION-NEXT STEPS

"THEN GOD SAID, 'LET US MAKE MAN IN OUR IMAGE, ACCORDING TO OUR LIKENESS; LET THEM HAVE DOMINION OVER THE FISH OF THE SEA, OVER THE BIRDS OF THE AIR, AND OVER THE CATTLE, OVER ALL THE EARTH AND OVER EVERY CREEPING THING THAT CREEPS ON THE EARTH.'"

–GENESIS 1:26 (NKJV)

DEVOTIONAL READING

JOSEPH'S LIFE SHOWS US THAT INFLUENCE IS NOT ABOUT POWER—IT'S ABOUT PURPOSE. HE DIDN'T FIGHT FOR FAME. HE STAYED FAITHFUL AND LET GOD PROMOTE HIM. WHEN FAMINE HIT EGYPT, JOSEPH LED WITH WISDOM, NOT PRIDE. HE USED HIS POSITION TO HELP OTHERS, NOT TO BUILD HIS NAME. THAT'S WHAT REAL KINGDOM INFLUENCE LOOKS LIKE—LEADING WITH LOVE AND SERVICE.

DOMINION DOESN'T MEAN DOMINATING PEOPLE. IT MEANS BRINGING ORDER, PEACE, AND BLESSING TO THE WORLD AROUND US. JOSEPH DIDN'T USE HIS AUTHORITY TO HARM—HE USED IT TO PROTECT. HE STORED FOOD FOR EGYPT AND SURROUNDING NATIONS. HIS LEADERSHIP SAVED LIVES AND REVEALED GOD'S HEART FOR WISE STEWARDSHIP.

OUR AUTHORITY COMES FROM GOD. JESUS SAID IN MATTHEW 28:18 THAT ALL AUTHORITY BELONGS TO HIM. AND ACTS 1:8 SAYS WE'LL RECEIVE POWER THROUGH THE HOLY SPIRIT. THIS KIND OF AUTHORITY ISN'T EARNED THROUGH STATUS—IT'S LIVED OUT THROUGH OBEDIENCE. LIKE JOSEPH, WE CARRY GOD'S PRESENCE AND POWER WHEN WE WALK IN HUMILITY.

Today,

WHERE HAS GOD GIVEN YOU INFLUENCE RIGHT NOW?

_____
_____
_____
_____
_____
_____

Today,

HOW ARE YOU USING YOUR GIFTS TO BLESS OTHERS?

_____
_____
_____
_____
_____
_____

Today,

WHAT AREA OF YOUR LEADERSHIP NEEDS MORE HUMILITY AND PRAYER?

_____
_____
_____
_____
_____
_____

**ASK GOD FOR INSIGHT:
PRAY FOR CLARITY ON
HOW TO LEAD WITH
PURPOSE WHERE YOU
ARE.**

_____
_____
_____
_____
_____
_____

**ACT WITH INTEGRITY:
CHOOSE TO DO WHAT
IS RIGHT, EVEN WHEN
IT'S HARD.**

_____
_____
_____
_____
_____
_____

**SERVE FIRST: USE YOUR
LEADERSHIP THIS WEEK
TO LIFT SOMEONE ELSE
UP.**

_____
_____
_____
_____
_____
_____

**STAY FAITHFUL IN THE HIDDEN
PLACES—GOD WILL REVEAL YOU
IN HIS TIME.**

SCRIPTURE MEDITATION

"THEN GOD BLESSED THEM, AND GOD SAID TO THEM, 'BE FRUITFUL AND MULTIPLY; FILL THE EARTH AND SUBDUE IT...'"
—GENESIS 1:28 (NKJV)

MEDITATION REFLECTION

FROM THE BEGINNING, GOD GAVE HIS PEOPLE INFLUENCE TO STEWARD, NOT TO ABUSE. JOSEPH UNDERSTOOD THIS WELL. EVEN WHEN HE HAD POWER, HE CHOSE SERVICE. HIS STORY REMINDS US THAT GOD PROMOTES THOSE WHO SERVE WITH EXCELLENCE AND STAY GROUNDED IN CHARACTER.

WALKING IN KINGDOM DOMINION MEANS LEADING WITH CARE, WISDOM, AND VISION. YOU DON'T NEED A TITLE TO INFLUENCE —YOU JUST NEED A WILLING HEART. LET GOD SHAPE YOUR LEADERSHIP SO IT REFLECTS HIS LOVE AND BRINGS LASTING IMPACT.

KEY POINTS

- INFLUENCE IS A GIFT TO SERVE, NOT TO CONTROL.
- TRUE DOMINION IS GROUNDED IN HUMILITY AND STEWARDSHIP.
- GOD HONORS FAITHFUL, SERVANT-HEARTED LEADERSHIP.

DEAR GOD,
THANK YOU FOR THE
OPPORTUNITY TO INFLUENCE
OTHERS FOR YOUR KINGDOM.
HELP ME WALK IN HUMILITY,
SERVE WITH LOVE, AND LEAD
WITH WISDOM. SHAPE MY HEART
TO REFLECT YOURS. TEACH ME TO
MANAGE WHAT YOU'VE
ENTRUSTED TO ME WITH CARE
AND PURPOSE. MAY MY
LEADERSHIP BLESS OTHERS AND
BRING YOU GLORY.
IN JESUS' NAME, AMEN.

JOURNAL REFLECTION-NEXT STEPS

Journal Reflection-Next Steps

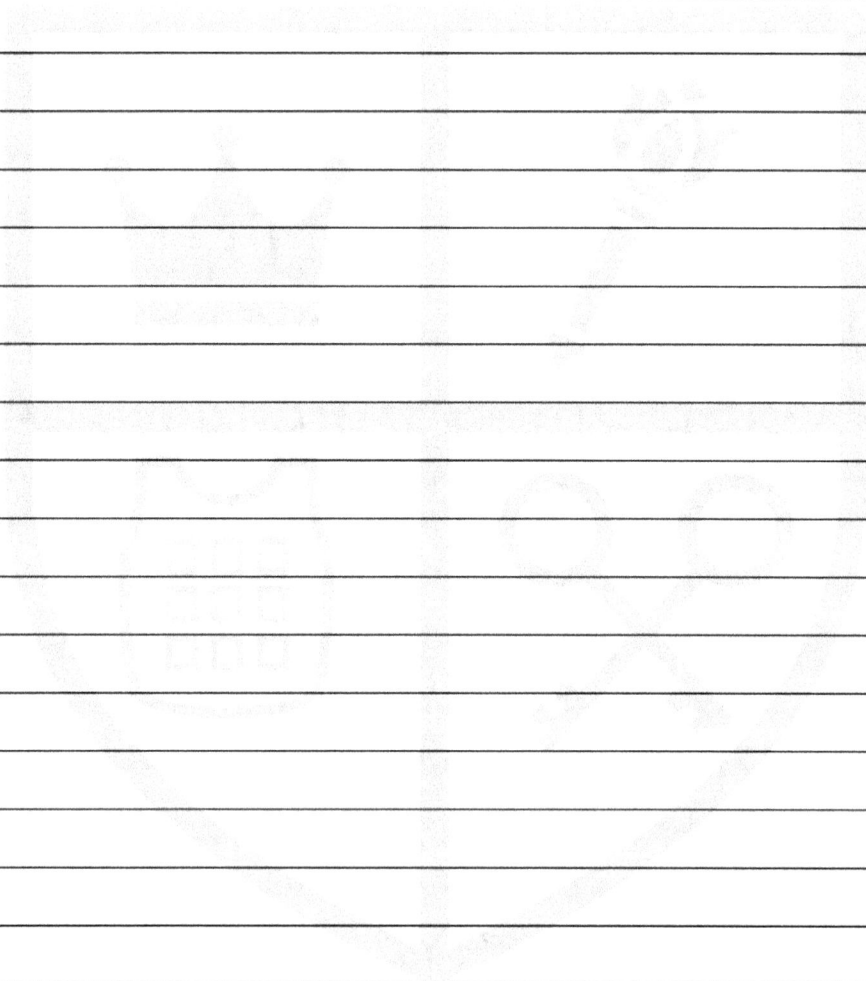

"BUT YOU SHALL RECEIVE POWER WHEN THE HOLY SPIRIT HAS COME UPON YOU; AND YOU SHALL BE WITNESSES TO ME... TO THE END OF THE EARTH."

–ACTS 1:8 (NKJV)

DEVOTIONAL READING

JOSEPH'S LIFE REMINDS US THAT BOLDNESS AND HUMILITY GO HAND IN HAND. HE WASN'T RECKLESS, BUT HE WAS COURAGEOUS. WHEN PHARAOH ASKED HIM TO INTERPRET A DREAM, JOSEPH POINTED TO GOD AND DELIVERED A BOLD PLAN. HE DIDN'T SHRINK BACK—HE STEPPED UP WITH WISDOM AND FAITH.

GOD GIVES US INFLUENCE NOT FOR FAME, BUT FOR SERVICE. PROVERBS 3:3-4 REMINDS US TO WEAR MERCY AND TRUTH LIKE A NECKLACE. WHEN WE LEAD WITH BOTH, PEOPLE TRUST US. JOSEPH'S BOLD LEADERSHIP SAVED NATIONS BECAUSE HE LISTENED TO GOD AND ACTED WITH COURAGE.

WHETHER YOU'RE LEADING A TEAM, A FAMILY, OR A CLASSROOM, YOUR LEADERSHIP MATTERS. EXCELLENCE IN SMALL THINGS OPENS BIG DOORS. PROVERBS 22:29 SAYS THOSE WHO EXCEL IN THEIR WORK WILL STAND BEFORE KINGS. FAITHFULNESS ALWAYS GETS GOD'S ATTENTION.

DAILY REFLECTION
Daily Reflection

Today,

**HOW CAN YOU LEAD
BOLDLY WITHOUT
BECOMING PRIDEFUL?**

_____
_____
_____
_____
_____

Today,

**WHAT DECISIONS DO
YOU NEED TO PRAY
ABOUT BEFORE
ACTING?**

_____
_____
_____
_____
_____

Today,

**WHO CAN YOU HELP
OR MENTOR WITH
YOUR INFLUENCE?**

_____
_____
_____
_____

BE COURAGEOUS: TAKE ONE BOLD STEP THIS WEEK TOWARD YOUR GOD-GIVEN CALLING.

_____
_____
_____
_____
_____
_____
_____

PRAY FIRST: ASK FOR GOD'S WISDOM BEFORE MAKING BIG DECISIONS.

_____
_____
_____
_____
_____
_____

LEAD WITH GRACE: USE YOUR INFLUENCE TO LIFT OTHERS UP, NOT TEAR THEM DOWN.

_____
_____
_____
_____
_____
_____

YOUR ATTITUDE IN THE WAITING DETERMINES YOUR ALTITUDE IN THE PROMOTION.

SCRIPTURE MEDITATION

"HAVE I NOT COMMANDED YOU? BE STRONG AND OF GOOD COURAGE... FOR THE LORD YOUR GOD IS WITH YOU WHEREVER YOU GO."
—JOSHUA 1:9 (NKJV)

MEDITATION REFLECTION

COURAGE IN LEADERSHIP DOESN'T MEAN LOUD OR FORCEFUL—IT MEANS FIRM IN FAITH AND STEADY IN PURPOSE. JOSEPH DIDN'T RUSH. HE WAITED ON GOD'S TIMING AND STEPPED FORWARD WHEN THE MOMENT WAS RIGHT. HIS SUCCESS WAS ROOTED IN TRUST AND STRATEGY.

LEADERSHIP THAT HONORS GOD IS BOTH STRONG AND GENTLE. IT'S CONFIDENT YET KIND. LET GOD SHAPE YOUR HEART AS YOU INFLUENCE OTHERS. BOLD OBEDIENCE WILL LEAD TO BREAKTHROUGHS—NOT JUST FOR YOU, BUT FOR THOSE YOU SERVE.

KEY POINTS

- BOLDNESS AND HUMILITY MUST WORK TOGETHER.
- WISE LEADERSHIP TAKES PRAYER AND PREPARATION.
- YOUR OBEDIENCE CAN UNLOCK PURPOSE FOR OTHERS.

DEAR GOD,
GIVE ME BOLDNESS TO
FOLLOW YOUR LEAD AND
HUMILITY TO GIVE YOU ALL
THE GLORY. HELP ME USE MY
INFLUENCE TO LIFT OTHERS
UP AND TO STAND STRONG
FOR WHAT'S RIGHT. WHEN I
FEEL AFRAID, REMIND ME
THAT YOU GO BEFORE ME.
MAY MY LEADERSHIP ALWAYS
REFLECT YOUR HEART.
IN JESUS' NAME, AMEN.

JOURNAL REFLECTION-NEXT STEPS
Journal Reflection-Next Steps

_____
_____
_____
_____
_____
_____
_____
_____
_____
_____
_____
_____
_____
_____
_____
_____
_____
_____
_____
_____
_____
_____
_____

"AND WHATEVER YOU DO, DO IT HEARTILY, AS TO THE LORD AND NOT TO MEN, KNOWING THAT FROM THE LORD YOU WILL RECEIVE THE REWARD OF THE INHERITANCE; FOR YOU SERVE THE LORD CHRIST."

–COLOSSIANS 3:23–24 (NKJV)

DEVOTIONAL READING

GOD IS RAISING UP LEADERS WHO CARRY HIS HEART INTO EVERYDAY SPACES—SCHOOLS, HOSPITALS, CITY HALLS, BUSINESSES. JOSEPH WAS ONE OF THESE LEADERS. THOUGH HE DIDN'T SERVE IN A TEMPLE, HIS LEADERSHIP WAS SPIRITUAL BECAUSE HE CARRIED GOD'S WISDOM INTO EGYPT'S MARKETPLACE. YOUR WORK, WHEN SURRENDERED TO GOD, BECOMES WORSHIP.

JOSEPH DIDN'T SEPARATE FAITH FROM FUNCTION. HIS ROLE IN GOVERNMENT BECAME A MISSION FIELD. HE SERVED WITH WISDOM AND STRATEGY, INFLUENCING ENTIRE NATIONS WHILE STAYING FAITHFUL TO GOD'S PROMISES. EVEN AT THE END OF HIS LIFE, HE POINTED HIS FAMILY BACK TO GOD'S COVENANT. THAT'S WHAT IT LOOKS LIKE TO LEAD WITH PURPOSE AND LEAVE A LEGACY OF FAITH.

LEADERSHIP IN THE MARKETPLACE STARTS WITH SEEING YOUR JOB AS A CALLING. WHETHER YOU'RE AN EMPLOYEE, MANAGER, STUDENT, OR ENTREPRENEUR, YOU ARE THERE ON ASSIGNMENT. GOD WANTS TO SHINE HIS LIGHT THROUGH YOUR EXCELLENCE, YOUR DECISIONS, AND YOUR KINDNESS.

Today,

HOW DO YOU VIEW YOUR CURRENT JOB OR ROLE AS A MINISTRY OPPORTUNITY?

_____
_____
_____
_____
_____
_____

Today,

WHAT LEGACY ARE YOU BUILDING THROUGH YOUR WORK AND LEADERSHIP?

_____
_____
_____
_____
_____
_____

Today,

WHERE CAN YOU APPLY MORE WISDOM AND FAITHFULNESS THIS WEEK?

_____
_____
_____
_____
_____
_____

SERVE FAITHFULLY: OFFER YOUR DAILY WORK TO GOD AS AN ACT OF WORSHIP.

_____

_____

_____

_____

_____

_____

PLAN WITH GOD: BRING YOUR BUSINESS OR CAREER GOALS BEFORE HIM IN PRAYER.

_____

_____

_____

_____

_____

_____

MENTOR SOMEONE: SHARE YOUR WISDOM WITH SOMEONE GROWING IN THEIR OWN CALLING.

_____

_____

_____

_____

_____

_____

LET YOUR LEADERSHIP BE A REFLECTION OF CHRIST'S LOVE.

SCRIPTURE MEDITATION

"WHATEVER YOU DO, DO IT HEARTILY, AS TO THE LORD AND NOT TO MEN."
—COLOSSIANS 3:23 (NKJV)

MEDITATION REFLECTION

GOD SEES YOUR FAITHFULNESS IN EVERY DETAIL. JOSEPH'S TASKS—MANAGING GRAIN, HELPING PHARAOH, ADVISING HIS FAMILY—WERE SACRED BECAUSE THEY WERE DONE WITH INTEGRITY. WHEN YOU BRING YOUR BEST, YOU REFLECT GOD'S EXCELLENCE. STEWARDSHIP ISN'T ABOUT HOW MUCH YOU HAVE, BUT HOW WELL YOU MANAGE WHAT'S IN YOUR HANDS.

MARKETPLACE MINISTRY MEANS LETTING YOUR FAITH SHOW IN BOARDROOMS, BREAK ROOMS, AND CLASSROOMS. LET YOUR WORDS BE FULL OF GRACE. LET YOUR LEADERSHIP BE FULL OF WISDOM. GOD IS WITH YOU AT EVERY DESK, EVERY MEETING, AND EVERY DECISION.

KEY POINTS

- YOUR JOB CAN BE HOLY GROUND WHEN IT'S SURRENDERED TO GOD.
- STRATEGY AND STEWARDSHIP ARE SPIRITUAL TOOLS.
- FAITHFUL WORK BUILDS LASTING LEGACY.

DEAR GOD,
THANK YOU FOR CALLING ME TO LEAD AND SERVE BEYOND THE CHURCH WALLS. HELP ME TO SEE MY WORK AS MINISTRY AND MY LEADERSHIP AS A CALLING. GIVE ME WISDOM IN EVERY TASK AND INTEGRITY IN EVERY CHOICE. MAY I BUILD SOMETHING THAT HONORS YOU AND BLESSES OTHERS. IN JESUS' NAME, AMEN.

JOURNAL REFLECTION-NEXT STEPS
Journal Reflection-Next Steps

"A GOOD MAN LEAVES AN INHERITANCE TO HIS CHILDREN'S CHILDREN, BUT THE WEALTH OF THE SINNER IS STORED UP FOR THE RIGHTEOUS."

– PROVERBS 13:22 (NKJV)

DEVOTIONAL READING

LEADERSHIP ISN'T JUST ABOUT SUCCESS—IT'S ABOUT STEWARDSHIP. JOSEPH DIDN'T JUST RISE TO POWER—HE USED HIS INFLUENCE TO PREPARE, PROTECT, AND BLESS. HIS WISDOM PRESERVED A NATION AND RESTORED HIS FAMILY. THAT'S KINGDOM STRATEGY—HEARING FROM GOD, ACTING WITH PURPOSE, AND LIFTING OTHERS ALONG THE WAY.

GOD GIVES YOU WISDOM NOT JUST FOR YOU, BUT FOR THOSE AROUND YOU. AS YOU BUILD AND LEAD, ASK: AM I MULTIPLYING BLESSINGS? AM I LEAVING BEHIND PEACE, FAITH, AND COURAGE? THE LEGACY YOU LEAVE IS SHAPED BY YOUR OBEDIENCE TODAY.

GOD HAS PLACED YOU WHERE YOU ARE ON PURPOSE. THE MARKETPLACE IS YOUR MISSION FIELD, AND YOUR LEADERSHIP MATTERS. YOU'RE NOT JUST WORKING—YOU'RE INFLUENCING. YOU'RE NOT JUST MANAGING—YOU'RE MENTORING. YOU'RE NOT JUST SUCCEEDING—YOU'RE STEWARDING SOMETHING ETERNAL.

DAILY REFLECTION
Daily Reflection

Today,

WHAT KIND OF LEGACY ARE YOU LEAVING THROUGH YOUR LEADERSHIP?

_____
_____
_____
_____
_____
_____
_____

Today,

HOW ARE YOU HELPING OTHERS GROW IN WISDOM, CHARACTER, OR FAITH?

_____
_____
_____
_____
_____
_____

Today,

WHAT'S ONE WAY YOU CAN PRACTICE KINGDOM STEWARDSHIP TODAY?

_____
_____
_____
_____
_____
_____

HONOR YOUR CALLING: REFLECT ON HOW YOUR CURRENT ROLE ADVANCES GOD'S KINGDOM.

_____
_____
_____
_____
_____
_____

BUILD WITH PURPOSE: SET A GOAL THAT ALIGNS YOUR LEADERSHIP WITH LASTING IMPACT.

_____
_____
_____
_____
_____

PRAY BOLDLY: ASK GOD TO ENLARGE YOUR TERRITORY WHILE KEEPING YOUR HEART HUMBLE.

_____
_____
_____
_____
_____

EVERY STEP OF FAITH MOVES YOU CLOSER TO YOUR KINGDOM ASSIGNMENT.

SCRIPTURE MEDITATION

"LET YOUR LIGHT SO SHINE BEFORE MEN, THAT THEY MAY SEE YOUR GOOD WORKS AND GLORIFY YOUR FATHER IN HEAVEN."
–MATTHEW 5:16 (NKJV)

MEDITATION REFLECTION

THE LIGHT YOU SHINE AT WORK, IN YOUR FAMILY, OR IN LEADERSHIP IS A WITNESS TO GOD'S GRACE. JOSEPH LED WITH WISDOM, HUMILITY, AND COURAGE. HE DIDN'T NEED A PULPIT– HIS LIFE PREACHED GOD'S GOODNESS. YOU CARRY THAT SAME CALL.

YOUR LEADERSHIP IS A LAMP. KEEP IT BURNING BRIGHT WITH PRAYER, COMPASSION, AND FAITH. AS YOU BUILD, SERVE, AND LEAD, REMEMBER–YOUR LIGHT POINTS PEOPLE TO THE ONE WHO CALLED YOU.

KEY POINTS

- JOSEPH'S STRATEGY SAVED LIVES. YOUR LEADERSHIP CAN TOO.
- KINGDOM LEADERS BUILD WITH ETERNITY IN MIND.
- YOUR LIGHT MATTERS–SHINE IT BOLDLY AND HUMBLY.

DEAR LORD,
THANK YOU FOR TRUSTING ME WITH INFLUENCE. HELP ME TO LEAD WITH INTEGRITY, TO SERVE WITH JOY, AND TO BUILD WITH FAITH. LET MY WORK REFLECT YOUR GOODNESS. HELP ME LEAVE A LEGACY OF WISDOM, LOVE, AND TRUTH. MAY EVERYTHING I DO BRING YOU GLORY AND DRAW OTHERS CLOSER TO YOU.
IN JESUS' NAME, AMEN.

JOURNAL REFLECTION-NEXT STEPS
Journal Reflection-Next Steps

_____
_____
_____
_____
_____
_____
_____
_____
_____
_____
_____
_____
_____
_____
_____
_____
_____
_____
_____
_____

JOURNAL REFLECTION
Journal Reflection

_____
_____
_____
_____
_____
_____
_____
_____
_____
_____
_____
_____
_____
_____
_____
_____
_____
_____
_____
_____
_____
_____

JOURNAL REFLECTION
Journal Reflection

JOURNAL REFLECTION

Journal Reflection

JOURNAL REFLECTION
Journal Reflection

JOURNAL REFLECTION
Journal Reflection

JOURNAL REFLECTION
Journal Reflection

JOURNAL REFLECTION
Journal Reflection

_____

_____

_____

_____

_____

_____

_____

_____

_____

_____

_____

_____

_____

_____

_____

_____

_____

_____

_____

_____

_____

_____

_____

ACKNOWLEDGEMENTS
Acknowledgements

First and foremost, we give all glory and honor to God—the Author and Finisher of our faith. These Joseph books are not just a collection of principles and stories; they are prophetic blueprints born in the secret place, shaped through obedience, and sealed by grace. Every page reflects His wisdom, His presence, and His Kingdom purpose.

To our families—thank you for your unwavering love and sacrificial support. To our beloved spouses, Pam and Michael, your steadfast commitment and prayer covering have been pillars of strength throughout this journey. To our children, your encouragement, grace, and quiet inspiration remind us of the next generation we are building for.

To one another—as co-authors, co-laborers, and co-founders of the Global Joseph Initiative, thank you for walking this journey in step with the Spirit and in unity of vision. It is an honor to serve together in raising up modern-day Josephs—leaders of influence, integrity, and prophetic authority—across every sphere of society.

To our spiritual mentors, prayer warriors, and apostolic voices—you helped birth this work in the Spirit. Your wisdom, intercession, and timely words of encouragement have strengthened us in ways words cannot express.

To our creative and technical team—editors, designers, formatters, and publishing partners—thank you for your excellence. Our behind-the-scenes work helped transform vision into reality, and your attention to detail has made this series both beautiful and accessible.

To our dear friends, readers, ministry partners, and fellow visionaries—thank you for your prayers, support, and belief in this work. You are part of this story, and we are grateful for your companionship on this Kingdom jour

And to you, our readers—whether you are in the pit, the prison, or the palace—know that you were never forgotten by God. May this series equip you to rise with bold faith, wisdom, and divine strategy. May the Spirit of Joseph rest upon you as you lead with integrity, steward with excellence, and transform your sphere of influence.

If this book has impacted you, please consider leaving a review online. Your testimony not only encourages us—it helps others discover the message and find their own path to purpose.

With deepest gratitude and Kingdom love,

Darrell "Coach D" Andrews & Dr. Shannon A. Austin

Darrell "Coach D" Andrews

Darrell "Coach D" Andrews is a dynamic minister, bestselling author, and visionary thought leader who brings bold faith, real-world wisdom, and contagious passion to every platform he touches. As a marketplace minister, he equips leaders to activate their God-given purpose—empowering them to lead with conviction, courage, and Kingdom strategy.

With over two decades of global impact, Coach D has served as a transformational force in Fortune 500 companies, educational institutions, government agencies, and faith-based organizations across North America and beyond. His presentations blend motivation, strategy, and spiritual insight, offering a holistic approach to leadership, reinvention, and cultural transformation.

Coach D holds the prestigious CSP (Certified Speaking Professional) designation, a distinction earned by fewer than 600 speakers worldwide. From post-pandemic leadership and self-care systems to Kingdom entrepreneurship and personal reinvention, Coach D releases more than motivation—he births movement.

He is a devoted husband of 30 years and proud father of four, modeling perseverance, humility, and unwavering faith in God. His voice is a prophetic trumpet calling leaders into alignment with Heaven's blueprint for transformation and revival.

Books by Darrell "Coach D" Andrews:
- The Purpose Living Teen: A Teen's Guide to Living Your Dreams
- Believing the HYPE: Seven Keys to Motivating Students of Color
- The Parent As Coach: Developing a Family Dream Team
- How to Find Your Passion and Make a Living at It
- Reinvention: The Pathway to Job Search Success
- The Self-Care Movement
- Post-Pandemic Leadership: The Key to Recruitment and Retention
- Featured in Chicken Soup for the African-American Soul ("5 Garbage Bags and a Dream")

Through these works, Coach D continues to uplift and equip diverse audiences with strategies that merge Kingdom values and practical application—mobilizing the next generation of purpose-driven leaders to step boldly into their divine assignments.

DR. SHANNON A. AUSTIN, PH.D., M.S., B.S.

Dr. Austin is a prophetic voice, thought leader, and spirit-empowered intercessor called to advance the Kingdom of God through prayer, leadership, and transformational ministry. Raised in the Catholic tradition and radically transformed by the power of the Holy Spirit, Dr. Austin carries a mantle of healing, deliverance, and strategic activation for leaders, families, and intercessory teams. Her ministry is marked by an unwavering devotion to prayer, deep intimacy with God, and a heart for restoration and identity alignment.

She holds a Ph.D. in Instructional Management and Leadership, an M.S. in Rehabilitation Counseling, and a triple-major B.S. in Business Administration, Organizational Leadership, and Social & Behavioral Science. Her educational background blends research-backed insights with real-world strategies to help individuals build resilience and achieve lasting success.

Shannon Austin has over 20 years of experience in workforce development, vocational rehabilitation, and human resources; she has dedicated her career to empowering others, fostering resilience, and creating innovative communities and workplaces. Her deep commitment to authenticity and empowerment is reflected in her company's core values of compassion, growth, community, and excellence.

She is a devoted wife of 35 years and proud mother of five, fully understanding the challenges of balancing personal and professional life while staying anchored in the Word of God. Her writings and ministry invite readers into a deeper walk with Christ.

Books by Dr. Shannon A. Austin:
- The Strength Within: Unlocking the Secrets of Resilience
- Unlocking Your Potential: Transforming Your Life with the Eight Pillars of Self-Care
- The Roadmap to Success: Strategic Life Planning for the 12 Areas of Life
- Family Is a Mosaic Picture: A Journey Through Brokenness, Belonging, and Becoming in the Hands of the Master Craftsman

Dr. Austin writes to inspire readers to trust in God's plan, embrace spiritual maturity, and pursue their God-given purpose with boldness. With a compassionate heart and a steadfast belief that every person has a role in God's redemptive story, she continues to build bridges of healing, hope, and purpose through her books, teachings, and prayer ministry.

CO-FOUNDERS OF THE GLOBAL JOSEPH INITIATIVE

Darrell "Coach D" Andrews and Dr. Shannon A. Austin are the visionary co-founders of the Global Joseph Initiative (globaljosephinitiative.org), a faith-based movement committed to raising up modern-day Josephs—leaders of influence, integrity, and prophetic authority—who transform culture in government, business, education, media, ministry, and beyond.

The Global Joseph Initiative equips faith-driven leaders with prophetic vision, practical tools, and spiritual wisdom to lead during seasons of both famine and abundance. Through devotionals, training, summits, and coaching, this initiative commissions Kingdom leaders to steward resources, unlock innovation, and lead cultural reformation through the Spirit of Joseph.

To learn more, partner with the movement, or invite Darrell or Shannon to speak, visit www.globaljosephinitiative.org or email info@globaljosephinitiative.org.

Co-Authored Series

Marketplace Leadership Series
- Joseph and Marketplace Ministry: Leadership, Entrepreneurship, and Kingdom Impact
- Joseph's Mantle and Marketplace Ministry: A 30-Day Devotional for Kingdom Leaders

Joseph Leadership for Emerging Voices
- Joseph & Marketplace Ministry: A Simple Guide to Kingdom Leadership
- Joseph & Marketplace Ministry Devotional: A 30-Day Guide to Living Your Calling

www.ingramcontent.com/pod-product-compliance
Lightning Source LLC
LaVergne TN
LVHW081332060426

835513LV00014B/1262